INSTRUCTIONAL DEVELOPMENT
— STEP BY STEP

INSTRUCTIONAL DEVELOPMENT
— STEP BY STEP

Six Easy Steps for Developing
Lean, Effective, and
Motivational Instruction

John S. Hoffman, PhD

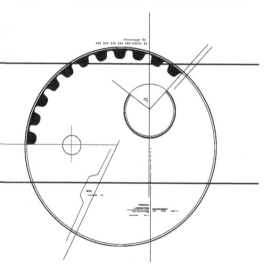

iUniverse, Inc.
Bloomington

iUniverse books may be ordered through booksellers or by contacting:

iUniverse
1663 Liberty Drive
Bloomington, IN 47403
www.iuniverse.com
1-800-Authors (1-800-288-4677)

Because of the dynamic nature of the Internet, any Web addresses or links contained in
this book may have changed since publication and may no longer be valid. The views
expressed in this work are solely those of the author and do not necessarily reflect the views
of the publisher, and the publisher hereby disclaims any responsibility for them.

Any people depicted in stock imagery provided by Thinkstock are models,
and such images are being used for illustrative purposes only.

Certain stock imagery © Thinkstock.

ISBN: 978-1-4759-8920-5 (sc)
ISBN: 978-1-4759-8921-2 (e)

Library of Congress Control Number: 2013908170

Printed in the United States of America

iUniverse rev. date: 5/13/2013

Contents

Preface

This book is a follow-on companion to my book, *Instructional Design—Step by Step: Nine Easy Steps for Designing Lean, Effective, and Motivational Instruction.* Instructional development is the activity that follows instructional design and is where the actual training deliverables are "fleshed out" by writers, instructional developers, and others, in accordance with the instructional design document. This book was written for three main audiences:

- those who are relatively new to the role of instructional development
- those who have been tasked with developing training or education that has been designed by an instructional designer who do not have a background or formal education in instructional design or development
- those who have some background or experience in instructional design and development who: (1) want to expand their skills in certain areas, such as performing content analysis to identify all required information for an instructional objective, writing instructional text using strategies that match the type of information being taught, and writing outstanding slides/pages/screens and corresponding titles or headings. It is also for those who just want an organized, concise, proven, and simple approach to instructional development

In this book, I have tried to distill my thirty-plus years of experience in developing education and training, my university degree in instructional design, and my sitting at the feet of some of the founding fathers in human performance improvement into a simple, straightforward, step-by-step process for *developing* instruction and training (see my other book referenced above to learn how to *design* instruction and training).

This book is not intended as a comprehensive treatment of the field of instructional development or technical writing. Rather, it is designed to teach a newcomer, in simple, understandable terms, how to craft effective, efficient, and successful instruction.

This book is not an academic tome; rather, it is a practitioner's guide. As such, I will be your personal mentor and tutor. I will teach you in the simplest way I know the minimum information and skills you will need to develop sound instructional deliverables, given an instructional design document or course outline and objectives.

The process I teach is not an unproven, abstract, or theoretical musing. I believe it is the quickest, most concise, and most direct way to develop effective instruction. I have practiced and refined this approach in numerous real-life projects with many clients on tasks and subject material ranging from the simple to the complex, from soft skills to the highly technical, covering a wide range of disciplines. In short, in this book, I have condensed all my wisdom, knowledge, and skill to its most essential elements and have packaged it into a simple step-by-step approach to instructional development.

Acknowledgments

Many people have influenced my thinking, insights, and understanding of instructional design and development throughout the years. In addition to the fundamentals that I acquired from earning a doctorate degree in instructional design, my insights have been greatly expanded upon by the likes of Joe Harless, Robert Horn, Bob Mager, Ruth Clark, and other giants in the field whose courses, seminars, books, and lectures matured my understanding and skill in human performance improvement. To each of them, I express my sincere gratitude.

To the many clients I have worked with during the last three decades, I express my gratitude for the opportunity to test, apply, and refine my approach to instructional design.

Finally, I acknowledge that no book is a solo effort. I am grateful to all of the professionals at iUniverse who have applied their skill and craft to make this book a reality.

Introduction and Overview

Welcome! You are about to learn how to develop instruction and training that is easy to understand, concise, effective, and rewarding. I have designed this book following the same process that I teach in my companion book, *Instructional Design—Step by Step: Nine Easy Steps for Designing Lean, Effective, and Motivational Instruction*. I hope, then, you will experience firsthand the benefits of following this approach.

Because this book is the second in a two-book series, I strongly recommend that you read my first book before reading this book. This book assumes that you know, for example:

- The fundamental principles of learning, cognition, and memory
- Common learning taxonomies (including those of Horn, Bloom, and Gagne)
- How to perform instructional analysis, content analysis, content sequencing, and several other techniques and principles used in instructional design

Why do you need to be grounded in instructional design to develop training materials? Because you will be refining the high-level instructional design that the instructional designer created when you develop your training materials. In other words, instructional *developers* do perform instructional design, just within a narrower scope and context. This is an insight that many developers are unaware. Anytime you create an instructional presentation, you are designing instruction—or, at least you should be.

In this book, only the minimum, essential information and skills are presented. This will keep you focused on the essential elements—no fluff is included here. After you understand the key principles and practices that make up this cognitive infrastructure, you will have an organized mental framework on which to venture out and assimilate the larger body of information that is available on this subject.

I have divided this book into two parts:

Part 1 presents a step-by-step approach to instructional development. It begins with an overview of the six steps of instructional development, which is followed by a detailed discussion of each step in individual chapters. Each of these steps is presented in its simplest terms and is supported by numerous examples, tables, and succinct lists. Part 1 has nine chapters.

Part 2 is a detailed discussion of how to create instructionally sound slides, screens, and frames—the smallest chunks of instruction that are presented at a time to students. More specifically, it presents several principles for creating effective titles for slides, screens, and frames; discusses how and where to create transitional slides, screens, and frames; and presents sixteen principles for designing, laying out, and structuring content. Part 2 has two chapters.

At the end of each chapter, I have included a series of checkpoint questions that will test your understanding of the key concepts and techniques found within that chapter. Each question is followed by the correct answer and detailed explanations. By answering these questions, you will quickly identify any gaps in your understanding, and you will know exactly what material you need to revisit.

Objectives of this book

This book, having been designed using the instructional design process taught in my companion book, would not be complete without a formal list of objectives. You can find more detailed objectives at the end of each chapter in the chapter summary.

Upon completion of this book, you should be able to

- define instructional development and explain how it is a continuation and refinement of the instructional design;
- given an instructional design document, create (write or author) the final course presentations, activities, and other deliverables by following the six steps of instructional development:
    1. Perform an analysis of the objectives to determine all enabling content.
    2. Classify information into its type and create corresponding instructional presentations.
    3. Create the remaining instructional events and finalize the topic.
    4. Create scripts (for technology-based training).
    5. Perform a quality check on the training materials.
    6. Pilot and revise all course materials.
- list and explain the principles for creating effective titles for slides, screens, and frames;
- define transitional slides, screens, and frames; explain their importance; and describe how they should be designed; and
- list and describe sixteen principles for creating outstanding slides, screens, and frames.

PART 1.

Developing Outstanding Training Materials

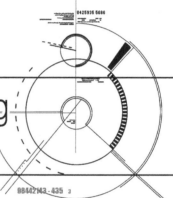

Overview of Part 1

Part 1 is a short course on how to *develop* outstanding training, given an instructional design document or high-level design. It describes the six major steps of instructional development and teaches critical skills, such as how to

- perform an analysis of the objectives to determine all of the enabling content,
- classify information into its type,
- design information presentations that match the information's type,
- create instructional events,
- finalize topics and lessons, and
- validate, quality check, pilot, and revise course materials.

After you complete part 1, you should be able to

- list and perform the six major steps for creating outstanding instructional materials:
    1. Analyze the objectives to determine all enabling content.
    2. Classify information into its type and create corresponding instructional presentations.
    3. Create the remaining instructional events and finalize the topic.
    4. Create scripts (for technology-based training)
    5. Perform a quality check on the training materials.
    6. Pilot and revise all course materials.

Part 1 has nine chapters.

What Is Instructional Development?

Instructional development is the set of activities required to create the instructional materials that were specified and prescribed by the instructional design document—the blueprints of the training. It is the construction phase of the training project.

Instructional developers are like builders and skilled craftsmen. They

- take the blueprints defined by the architect,
- analyze the blueprints further to determine the specific detailed elements that need to be constructed,
- determine how those elements will fit together,
- build the elements and the structure, and
- perform quality checks.

Your goal in instructional development is to

- develop training deliverables that are instructionally sound, effective, and motivational, and
- fulfill the plan, vision, structure, and requirements that were specified in the instructional design document.

The output of instructional development is a complete master copy of the training materials in final form (hardcopy, Flash files, web pages, instructor guides, and so forth), ready for installation and delivery to students using the delivery system (or systems) specified in the instructional design document.

Who Is Involved in Developing Training?

Developing training typically requires the skills of many different professionals, such as

- content developers (writers);
- editors;
- graphic artists;
- authoring-language software experts (for technology-based training);
- accessibility experts and compliance personnel;
- testing personnel who check that all functions, interactions, and links work as specified in the final training (for technology-based training);
- IT specialists, for specialized online delivery systems or technology driven instructional events (such as Flash developers);
- administrative specialists who post and activate the training in learning management systems (LMS) for enrollment, delivery, and tracking; and

- project managers (PMs) who manage and oversee all design and development personnel and activities and who interface with the business and the client

This book was written for content developers and writers—the individuals who craft the instructional presentations (verbal, online, multimedia, or written) of the training. It is *not* a course on writing, grammar, or style, nor does it cover the other areas of expertise represented by this list of professionals.

Why Is Instructional Development Important?

The most brilliant architectural blueprints for a spectacular new skyscraper will fail to be realized if those who construct the skyscraper do not

- know how to understand and interpret the blueprints,
- follow and adhere to those plans, and
- build using proven, high-quality construction techniques with high-quality materials.

Likewise, the best instructional design, if not properly developed and implemented, will be made ineffective. Students learn by interacting with course materials in the context of the course delivery (classroom or technology based). This is where real learning occurs. If the detailed information presentations and student interactions in the training materials do not follow proven principles of learning and teaching, then learning will be compromised, impeded, or entirely frustrated.

Effective, lean, and motivational learning require both quality design and quality development (construction).

Isn't Developing Training Largely a Creative Task?

Although creativity is involved in developing certain course elements, such as instructional graphics, lively case studies, and interesting interactions, the majority of instructional development is *analytical* in nature. For example, two key tasks in instructional development are classifying chunks of information into their type and creating instructional presentations that employ instructional strategies specific to that type of information.

Skills and Attitudes That You Will Need as an Instructional Developer

To be a true professional instructional developer, you will need to possess or develop the following skills and attitudes:

- a desire to understand how humans learn
- a desire to understand and apply well known, proven principles of learning and teaching
- analytical reasoning and problem-solving ability
- the ability to handle complexity, uncertainty, and incomplete information
- the discipline necessary to rigorously follow instructional development methodology
- an ability to deal with things at both high levels and detailed levels
- attention to detail
- excellent teaming and communication skills
- great persistence, especially in following up and tracking down content and answers to questions about content with the subject matter experts (SMEs)
- skills specific to your specialty as a developer (such as writing, editing, graphics, multimedia development, and so forth)

Your Work Will Be on Display for Everyone to See!

As an instructional developer, what you produce is not passed off to other individuals, never to be seen by anyone else except by other professionals having specific expertise inside your company or organization. What you create are the end-deliverables for training—what students will see, interact with, and participate in. You are like an artist who is hanging up his painting for all to see.

If you are proud of what you have produced, this can be very rewarding. If you do not understand what it takes to make a great painting and discipline yourself to apply those principles and techniques, you might not be so proud of your work. By arming yourself with the principles and techniques taught in this book, you will always have reason to be very proud of what you produce.

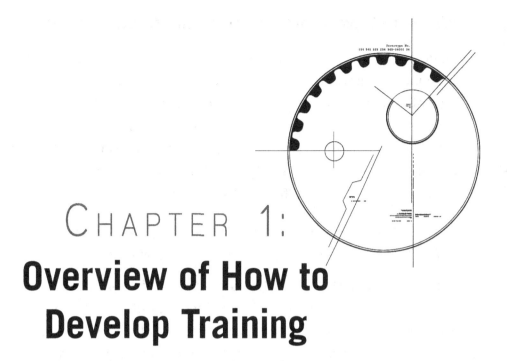

CHAPTER 1:
Overview of How to Develop Training

This chapter presents an overview of the instructional development process. It describes the major activities involved in developing training, including analyzing topic objectives to determine all of the enabling content for a topic; classifying information into its type; designing information presentations that match the information's type; creating exercises and other instructional events; finalizing the sequence of materials for a topic; creating scripts for technology-based training; performing a quality check on the training materials; and piloting and revising the course materials.

The Six Steps of the Instructional Development Process

Developing and building an outstanding training course from the specifications given in an instructional design document is not a chance event. It requires a disciplined, systematic approach to instructional development—one that uses a variety of skills that employ a variety of instructional analyses, writing, and micro-design tasks. The outcome of instructional development is the final course deliverables—typically, the final training course consisting of all of the course materials ready for publishing or delivery.

Assuming that you have the instructional design document, developing training is performed by carrying out the following six steps:

1. **Analyze the objectives to determine all enabling content:** Analyze the objectives to determine each objective's type (skill, knowledge, or attitude); then, complete the analysis of the objective using the analysis techniques appropriate for that type of objective. This results in a collection of all of the enabling content that must be taught for that objective. Repeat this task for each objective in the course.

2. **Classify information into its type and create corresponding instructional presentations:** For each type of enabling content, create the presentational materials following the instructional strategy that is appropriate for teaching that information type.

3. **Create the remaining instructional events and finalize the topic:** Create the exercises and other instructional events specified in the instructional design document, determine if any additional prerequisite information needs to be refreshed, and determine the overall sequence of all presentation and instructional events for the topic.

4. **Create scripts (for technology-based training):** Create scripts that specify all necessary text and design elements for a technology specialist in the delivery technology to create the instructional presentation or event.

5. **Perform a quality check on the training materials:** Perform a review to ensure that the content supports the objectives (no extraneous

content) and that all objectives have supporting content (no missing content), compare the training materials against the instructional design document and against a training checklist, and have the training materials reviewed by editors, testers, subject matter experts (SMEs), and others.

6.   **Pilot and revise all course materials:** Try out the course with students from the target audience, solicit feedback, and make any needed improvements.

Note: Throughout part 1, the terms *topic* and *lesson* are used interchangeably. They both refer to the smallest instructional sequence in a course that typically has an introduction, lesson content, activities, exercises, and a summary.

Step 1: Analyze the Objectives to Determine All Enabling Content

In the instructional design phase, instructional designers analyze the training requirements and create high-level course plans or blueprints.

During development, these plans are passed on to instructional developers who analyze the objectives and continue drilling down the instructional and content analyses to determine the complete body of detailed information that must be taught to achieve the topic's objectives. In step 1, all of the enabling information—every concept, fact, principle, structure, classification, process, and procedure required to master the objective—must be identified.

For information on how to perform instructional and content analyses, see chapters 8 through 10 in my companion book, *Instructional Design—Step by Step: Nine Easy Steps for Designing Lean, Effective, and Motivational Instruction*. Bloomington, IN: iUniverse, 2013.

Why Is Determining All of the Enabling Content During Instructional Development Necessary?

The short answer is because the analysis in the instructional design document probably did not drill down all the way to the most detailed level—the level of the target audience's entry-level skills and knowledge. To do so would have required long hours with subject matter experts (SMEs). All of the enabling content must be identified to know what must be taught in a given lesson or topic.

It is often more efficient to sketch out the high-level course design, structure, and content during the instructional design phase and then assign multiple developers to simultaneously create the course materials during the development phase of the project. This is especially true for large, complex courses.

To refer back to our analogy in the construction industry, an architect of a building does not typically specify how every cut should be made, where every hole should be drilled, or where every nail should be placed in the building's studs, joists, and rafters. Rather, carpenters and other trade professionals read the architect's blueprints, perform mental calculations, and make detailed decisions that comply with building codes and standard industry practices when they erect walls, floors, and roofs.

Why is determining all of the enabling content necessary? To obtain the same benefits as performing higher-level instructional and content analyses; namely, to systematically identify all of the enabling content, to structure information in a logical fashion, and to create lean, effective, and relevant instruction.

Ultimately, learning occurs at the lowest level of the analysis where each concept, principle, step, and so on are taught in a logical sequence. These individual chunks of information must therefore be systematically identified.

How to Determine All of the Enabling Content

This step requires two specific inputs from the instructional design document:

- the combined instructional and content analysis that were performed for this particular lesson or topic during the design phase
- the objectives for this lesson or topic

To perform this step in the development process:

1. Analyze the objectives using the skills, knowledge, and attitude (SKA) taxonomy to classify each objective as a skill, knowledge, or attitudinal objective.
2. Use the analysis techniques that are appropriate to each type of objective to drill down and further analyze the information.

The result is a collection of all of the detailed content that must be taught for each objective in each lesson.

In this step, the information is analyzed all the way down to the point at which any further analysis would only identify skills and information that are part of the assumed entry level knowledge and skills of your target audience.

Step 2. Classify Information into Its Type and Create Corresponding Instructional Presentations

In part 1, "Understanding How Humans Learn," in my companion book, *Instructional Design—Step by Step: Nine Easy Steps for Designing Lean, Effective, and Motivational Instruction*, you learned that you can classify all information into one of seven different types using Robert Horn's taxonomy.

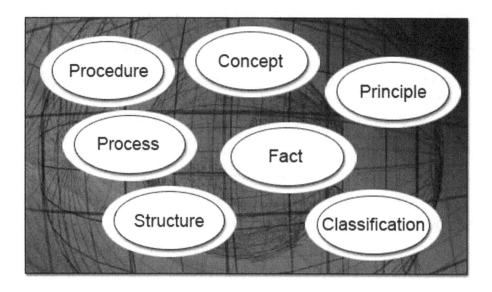

Figure 1. Robert Horn's seven information types

For review, here are Robert Horn's seven information types:

- procedures
- processes
- concepts
- principles
- facts
- structures
- classifications

In this step of the instructional development process, you classify each chunk of enabling information identified in step 1 according to its type. Then you design and create instructional presentations that employ research-based instructional strategies for teaching that type of information.

This means, for example, that the strategy for teaching concepts is different than the strategy for teaching procedures or the strategy for teaching facts. Each type of information has its own recommended instructional strategy for how to teach that *type* of information.

A lesson typically must teach many different types of information. Teach each type of information in the way prescribed by the instructional strategy for that type of information. These instructional strategies are discussed in part 1 of this book.

Why Is Classifying Information into Its Type and Creating Corresponding Instructional Presentations Important?

Learning is maximized when research-based principles and prescriptions are followed in teaching and presenting that information. These principles and prescriptions differ somewhat, depending on the type of information that is being taught.

For example, one type of information is a concept.

Here is an example of how *not* to teach a concept and how to fix it:

Suppose that your analysis showed that one of the enabling content concepts for a topic was the concept of a quadrahelion. A casual trainer might just provide a verbal definition and leave it at that:

"A quadrahelion is a four-strand helical complex that is linked together periodically by structures arranged in rectangles or squares."

This provides some information but leaves it to students' imaginations to really understand what it is. This concept would be better taught if the instructor also provided

- examples and non-examples of quadrahelions (perhaps using graphics),
- an expansion and deeper explanation of each of the critical attributes of quadrahelions and a comparison of these attributes to the attributes of other similar structures that are not quadrahelions, and
- an opportunity for students to practice identifying instances and non-instances of quadrahelions and receive detailed feedback and explanations of correct and incorrect classifications

Employing instructional strategies that are based on the information's type makes it much easier for students to learn and remember the information. On the other hand, failing to follow the recommended instructional strategies for the information's type will hinder or halt the learning of the information.

How to Classify Information into Its Type and Create Corresponding Instructional Presentations

To classify information into its type:

1. Study the definitions and examples given for each information type.

2. Determine the *purpose* for presenting this information to the student.

These steps will be discussed in more detail in part 1 of this book.

Here are some examples of classifying information into its type:

If the student needs to understand:
- how customer orders are received and processed, use a process.
- how to receive and process customer orders, use a procedure.
- which department handles which kind of complaint, use a classification.
- the client's business organization chart, use a structure.
- what e-commerce is, use a concept.
- who must sign off on the sales order, use a fact—unless, that is, certain rules or policies must be followed to determine who must sign off on the order, in which case use a principle.

To create a corresponding information presentation, follow the detailed prescriptions that are discussed later in part 1 for each type of information.

Step 3. Create the Remaining Instructional Events and Finalize the Topic

In this step, you create the exercises and the other instructional events that were given in the instructional design document for this topic, determine if any additional prerequisite information needs to be refreshed, and determine the overall sequence of all presentation and instructional events for the topic.

Examples of instructional events include exercises, role plays, group exercises, introductions, simulations, summaries, checkpoint questions, demonstrations, instructional games, quizzes, and so forth. To create the prescribed instructional events, you must often perform further research or analysis to identify the specific content for each event, such as the step-by-step instructions for an exercise.

This step is necessary even though the instructional events were already prescribed by the instructional design document because:

- the instructional design document only provides a high-level design for exercises and other instructional events; therefore, you must further analyze and design these activities to arrive at their specific content.
- design is a plan. You must still actually *create* or *write* the instructional events.
- sometimes during detailed analysis of the information during development, you recognize the need for an additional exercise, demonstration, or other instructional event that was not specified in the instructional design document. In this case, after obtaining approval for the activity from the instructional designer, create the design for the activity.

Refreshing Additional Prerequisite Information

When you continue the instructional and content analyses that were begun during instructional design, you might identify a need to refresh additional prerequisite information that was *not* already listed to be refreshed by the instructional design document. This prerequisite information might have been taught in a previous lesson, or it might be part of the assumed entry-level knowledge and skills of your audience. You must decide if it needs to be refreshed before you present the main lesson content.

In deciding what information to refresh, you should ask yourself, "How likely are students to remember the information at the level of detail that is required in this lesson?" If they are not likely to remember, then consider providing a brief refresher or review of the information or consider including an activity that refreshes the information.

Finalizing the Sequence of All Lesson Materials

The next task in step 3 is to finalize the sequence of all of the information and instructional events for the lesson. This sequence should be a refinement of the sequence given in the instructional design document.

This step is necessary because, during development, you continue to drill down and analyze content until you have identified *all* of the enabling content for the lesson. This collection of detailed content must then be sequenced along with any other additional instructional events that you identify as necessary and have been approved by the instructional designer.

Step 4. Create Scripts (for Technology-Based Training)

Step 4 in the development process applies only to technology-based training, such as web-based training. For technology-based training, the instructional developer typically must create a script for each topic, lesson, or event. Scripts provide technology experts and other professionals with all the information they need, including the content and the descriptions of any interactions with students, to build the presentation or event.

Here are the entries that are typically included in scripts for web-based training

- the screen or event number
- the title to be displayed on the screen

- the type of screen (templates are usually created for each screen type)
- specifications for any graphics to be displayed on the screen
- the text to be displayed on the screen
- descriptions of any special interactions that the student can or must take on the screen
- graphic file names
- alt text descriptions for graphical accessibility compliance
- the instructional prompts that will tell the student what to do on that screen

Scripts for time-based, highly interactive, or media intensive events, such as Flash animations and interactions or video, have their own special requirements that can be specified by those who are experts in building or creating these types of interactions.

Scripts are typically created as shell documents or files. Developers place the information produced by the other steps in the instructional development process into the script format.

Step 5. Perform a Quality Check on the Training Materials

This step involves two tasks: Validating the materials and quality checking the materials.

Validating the materials is checking to see

- if all course materials support the objectives (no extraneous or unnecessary material has slipped into the course);
- if all objectives have supporting content (no missing content);
- if your materials "flesh out" (embody) the design specified in the instructional design document; and
- if all of the instructional *events* (activities, such a practice with feedback) are there that are needed to master the objectives.

Quality checking the course consists of

- reviewing your materials against an instructional development quality checklist;
- having an accessibility review performed to ensure that the course complies with accessibility requirements for the disabled;
- having a professional edit performed on all of your content for grammar, style, legal and trademark issues, and compliance with any organizational standards;
- having a functional test performed to test the navigation, links, and interactive features of online courses to ensure that they are functioning properly (for technology-based training);
- having the course reviewed by the instructional designer; and
- having the course reviewed by the subject matter experts for technical accuracy.

Step 6. Pilot and Revise All Course Materials

This final step in the development process involves two tasks: Piloting the course, and making revisions and improvements based on the pilot feedback. This step helps ensure that the course will be motivational, lean, and effective in achieving its goals.

Piloting the course is trying out the training on the target audience in preliminary training sessions and soliciting feedback using written assessments, interviews, surveys, or other evaluation techniques to see

- how well the course achieved its objectives
- where improvements need to be made
- how well students liked the course

Revising the course is making the needed improvements that were uncovered by the course pilots and peer and subject matter expert reviews.

Instructional Development Is a Continuation of the Instructional Design Process and a Refinement of the Instructional Design

In learning about the instructional development process, you might have been surprised about how many of the steps involved a continuation of the analysis and design activities that were either begun during instructional design or were prescribed there at a high level.

This is a key insight. Instructional developers are micro-instructional designers. They must know how to perform many of the same analysis and design techniques that instructional designers must know. However, they typically perform them at a lower level in the course, within the confines of the individual course modules, topics, and activities that were defined and sequenced in the instructional design document by the instructional designer.

If you do not know how to perform these design techniques and activities, you should read my companion book, *Instructional Design—Step by Step: Nine Easy Steps for Designing Lean, Effective, and Motivational Instruction*, before continuing this book. Part 1 assumes that you have read this book and understand instructional design.

Chapter Summary—Overview of How to Develop Training

This chapter presented an overview of the instructional development process. It described the major activities involved in developing training, including analyzing topic objectives to determine all of the enabling content for a topic; classifying information into its type; designing information presentations that match the information's type; creating exercises and other instructional events; finalizing the sequence of materials for a topic; creating scripts for technology-based training; performing a quality check on the training materials; and piloting and revising the course materials.

You should now be able to

- list the six steps of the instructional development process;
- for each of the following steps in the development process, state the purpose of that step, describe how it is carried out at a high level, and explain why that step is important
    1. Analyze the objectives to determine all enabling content,
    2. Classify information into its type and create corresponding instructional presentations,
    3. Create the remaining instructional events and finalize the topic,
    4. Create scripts (for technology-based training),
    5. Perform a quality check on the training materials,
    6. Pilot and revise all course materials, and
- describe how instructional development is a continuation and refinement of the instructional design.

Check Your Understanding

1. **Which of the following are steps in the instructional *development* (not design) process? (Select all that apply.)**
    A. Gather requirements
    B. Pilot and revise all course materials

C. Classify information into its type and create corresponding instructional presentations

D. Create the remaining instructional events and finalize the topic

E. Determine the instructional delivery system

F. Analyze the objectives to determine all enabling content

G. Determine the instructional delivery system

H. Create scripts (for technology-based training)

I. Perform a quality check on the training materials

2. **True or false? During instructional *development*, an instructional analysis is complete if it has been taken all the way down to the point at which any further analysis would only identify skills and information that are part of the assumed entry level knowledge and skills of your target audience.**

3. **True or false? An instructional design document typically specifies every last detail of the training.**

4. **True or false? The instructional developer uses two major inputs from the instructional design document as the starting point for further analysis: (1) the instructional and content analyses that were previously performed for this topic, and (2) the topic's objectives.**

5. **True or false? Instructional strategies for teaching information are the same, regardless of the type of information.**

6. **True or false? In teaching information, employing instructional strategies that are based on the type of information being taught make it much easier for students to learn and remember the information.**

7. **True or false? In classifying information into its type in preparation for creating corresponding instructional presentations, it is important to consider the *purpose* for presenting the information to the student.**

8. **True or false? During development, when you are finishing the analysis that was begun during instructional design, you might discover the need for an additional exercise, demonstration, or**

other instructional event that was not specified in the instructional design document.

9. **True or false? In deciding what prerequisite information needs to be refreshed, you should ask yourself, "How likely are students to remember the information at the level of detail that is required in this lesson?"**

10. **True or false? The principles for sequencing information at the unit, module, or course levels are different than the principles for sequencing information at the topic, lesson, or within-lesson levels.**

11. **True or false? Technology-based training requires an extra step during instructional development to write scripts that tell media and technology developers how to create the presentations or events.**

12. **In addition to validating the course materials, quality checking a course consists of which of the following activities? (Select all that apply.)**

    A. Performing a professional edit of all materials by professional editors for grammar, style, legal and trademark issues, and compliance with any organizational standards.

    B. Piloting the course on the target audience and evaluating the attainment of course objectives and soliciting feedback

    C. Performing an accessibility review to ensure that the course complies with accessibility requirements for the disabled

    D. Testing the navigation, links, and interactive features of online courses to ensure that they are functioning properly

    E. Having the course reviewed by peers and technical experts for a final check on course integrity, instructional effectiveness, and technical accuracy

    F. Revising the course to make needed improvements that were uncovered by the course pilots and peer and subject matter expert reviews

13. **True or false? Piloting the course is trying out the training on the target audience in preliminary training sessions and soliciting**

feedback using written assessments, interviews, surveys, or other evaluation techniques to see how well the course achieved its objectives, where improvements need to be made, and how well students liked the course.

14. **True or false? Instructional developers are micro-instructional designers.**

Answers

1. B, C, D, F, H, and I
2. True
3. False. The instructional design document specifies the course structure, instructional events, objectives, and so forth, but typically does not carry the instructional and content analyses all the way down to entry level skills and knowledge. Exceptions can occur, though, when (1) the course or content to be analyzed is small, and (2) when it is more efficient to complete the analysis with the SMEs all at once during the design phase than to require that instructional developers continue the analysis to the lower levels during the development phase of the project.
4. True
5. False. Instructional *principles* apply across the board, but instructional *strategies*—the elements required to teach the information and how best to sequence and present it—differ by the type of information (concept, fact, process, principles, procedure, structure, or classification).
6. True
7. True
8. True
9. True
10. False
11. True
12. A, C, D, and E
13. True
14. True. Instructional development is a continuation of the instructional design process and a refinement of the instructional design. Developers

must know how to perform many of the same design activities and techniques that instructional designers must know. However, they typically perform them at a lower level in the course, within the confines of the individual course modules, topics, and activities that were previously defined and sequenced in the instructional design document.

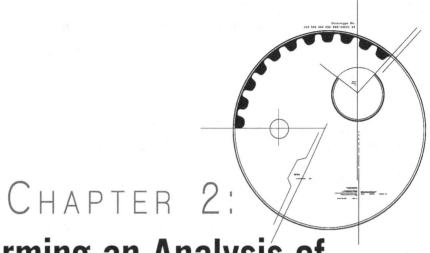

CHAPTER 2:

Performing an Analysis of the Objectives to Determine All Enabling Content

This chapter discusses how to perform an analysis of the objectives to determine all of the enabling content that is required for a lesson or topic. This is the first step in the instructional development process.

Where We Are At in the Instructional Development Process

This chapter discusses step 1 in the instructional development process: Perform an analysis of the objectives to determine all enabling content.

1. **Analyze the objectives to determine all enabling content.**
2. Classify information into its type and create corresponding instructional presentations.

3. Create the remaining instructional events and finalize the topic.
4. Create scripts (for technology-based training).
5. Perform a quality check on the training materials.
6. Pilot and revise all course materials.

Overview of How to Complete the Instructional and Content Analyses

The first task in developing a lesson or topic is to perform an analysis of the lesson objectives to determine all of the enabling content that must be taught in that lesson. This step requires two specific inputs from the instructional design document:

- the combined instructional and content analysis that were performed for this particular lesson or topic during the design phase, and
- the objectives for this lesson or topic.

To perform this step in the development process:

1. Analyze the objectives using the skills, knowledge, and attitude (SKA) taxonomy to classify each objective as a skill, knowledge, or attitudinal objective.
2. Use the analysis techniques that are appropriate to each type of objective to drill down and further analyze the information.

The result is a collection of all of the detailed content that must be taught for each objective in each lesson.

Note: In this step, the information is analyzed all the way down to the point at which any further analysis would only identify skills and information that are part of the assumed entry level knowledge and skills of your target audience.

Review of the Skills, Knowledge, and Attitude (SKA) Taxonomy

First, let us review the SKA taxonomy. SKA classifies all learning into three general categories.

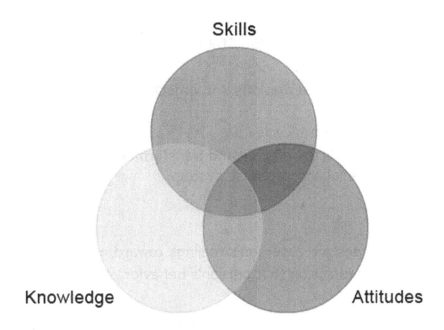

Figure 2. The Skills, Knowledge, and Attitude (SKA) taxonomy

Skill

Definition: Skills involve the performance of a task that produces an end result.

Examples

- Answer customer objections using the ABC methodology.
- Use the ABC ERP software application to send out requests for bids for new orders.
- Analyze a use case to identify potential programming objects.
- Determine the best approach for approaching executives in an enterprise to sell them e-business on demand.

Knowledge

Definition: Knowledge is the understanding, retention, and recall of information (concepts, facts, and so forth).

Examples

- List all fifty states in the United States.
- Define logical partitions.
- Show the UML representations for objects, messages, classes, and inheritance.
- Identify the parts of a bicycle.
- Describe how data is transferred and transformed from the point of entry to storage in the legacy database system.

Attitude

Definition: Attitudes are a person's feelings toward other people, groups, or things and their effect on that person's behavior.

Examples

- Voluntarily conform to accessibility guidelines.
- Value the opinions of others on the team.
- Complete all quality checkpoints without error.
- Speak out against sexual harassment when witnessing it in others.
- Submit a suggestion into the suggestion box twice a year.

For more information on SKA, see Chapter 3, "Learning Taxonomies and Their Application," in my companion book, *Instructional Design—Step by Step: Nine Easy Steps for Designing Lean, Effective, and Motivational Instruction*. Bloomington, IN: iUniverse, 2013.

Classifying Objectives Using SKA

To classify an instructional objective, identify the behavior or performance that is prescribed by the objective and consider the overall purpose of the objective.

The following table describes how to classify an objective:

If the behavior describes	Then the objective is	Example behaviors
The performance of a series of overt or covert steps that are used to produce an end result	A skill objective	Handle a customer service call Fix a machine. Answer customer objections to the closing of the sale. Determine the company's profit for the last quarter.
A performance (for example, list, state, describe, define, explain, and so forth) whose purpose is to indicate whether students comprehend or can recall specific knowledge	A knowledge objective	List all 15 parts of the XYZ widget. Define distributed computing. Fill in the names of the parts in the following exploded diagram of an air injector. Explain why compound interest is critical to increasing one's savings over the long term.
What the student will choose to say or do that are indicators of the student's feelings or regard toward other people, groups, or things	An attitudinal objective	Comply with the business casual dress code by wearing appropriate dress to work. Defend the free enterprise system when challenged by others. Support others expressing their opinions in team meetings even when they differ from your own.

After you have classified the objective into its SKA type, the next step is to determine which analysis technique you should use to further analyze the information. The type of analysis that you use to continue the analysis depends on the type of objective.

The following table describes which analysis techniques are used to analyze each of the three types of objectives:

Analysis Techniques Prescribed by the Type of Objectives		
Skill objectives	**Knowledge objectives**	**Attitudinal objectives**
Skills are analyzed by breaking them down into their component tasks, subtasks, and steps in a hierarchical fashion and are taught as procedures. This analysis procedure is called a task or instructional analysis. The enabling content must also be identified for each step using a procedure called content analysis.	Knowledge is analyzed by breaking it down into its component knowledge and is taught using presentation strategies appropriate to the specific type of knowledge (such as concepts, facts, principles). This analysis procedure is called a content analysis.	Attitudes are analyzed by clearly defining the attitude and identifying its indicator behaviors. This analysis is called an indicator behavior analysis.

Analyzing Skill Objectives

Skill objectives involve the performance of a task. Use instructional analysis to continue drilling down the analysis started in the instructional design document into its component subtasks until you eventually identify the individual discrete steps for performing the task. Then perform a content analysis on the steps to determine the enabling content for that procedure. The end result is the steps of one or more procedures and the supporting enabling content.

Here is an example of the beginning of an analysis of a skill objective:

Consider the objective, "Given a memory PTM and customer configuration requirements, install, configure, and test the PTM for proper functioning."

The first level of task and content analysis for this objective would result in enabling content and subskills such as

- how to install a memory PTM (this subtask needs further task analysis),
- how to configure a memory PTM (this subtask needs further task analysis),
- how to test the PTM (this subtask needs further task analysis),
- what is a memory PTM (depending on the complexity of this concept, this concept might need additional content analysis)?,
- what are customer configuration requirements (depending on the complexity of this information, this information might need additional content analysis)? and
- what should you do if something is not working correctly (depending on the complexity of this information, this information might need additional task and content analyses)?

How to perform task and content analyses are assumed entry level skills for this book. If you do not know how to perform these techniques, see part 2, "Creating Outstanding Instructional Designs," in my companion book, *Instructional Design—Step by Step: Nine Easy Steps for Designing Lean, Effective, and Motivational Instruction*. Bloomington, IN: iUniverse, 2013.

Analyzing Knowledge Objectives

To analyze knowledge objectives, use content analysis to drill down higher-level concepts and information into lower-level components. The end result is a hierarchy of information with the lowest-level concepts and information at the bottom of the hierarchy.

Consider the knowledge objective, "Define networks and describe fundamental network concepts, such as network control, network cabling, network topologies, the ISO model, and the different types of networks (LANS and WANS)."

Knowing how to perform content analysis is an assumed entry level skill for this book. If you do not know how to perform this technique, see chapter 10, "Identifying the Enabling Content," in my companion book, *Instructional Design—Step by Step: Nine Easy Steps for Designing Lean, Effective, and Motivational Instruction*. Bloomington, IN: iUniverse, 2013.

Here is how this knowledge objective was further analyzed using content analysis:

---

1 Fundamental network concepts
    1.1 Networking concepts
      1.1.1 Definition of a network
        1.1.1.1 Collection of interconnected hosts that share information
          1.1.1.1.1 Systems interconnected with wires or fibers
          1.1.1.1.2 Wires and fibers are attached to system adapter cards and other network components (hubs, routers, and switches)
          1.1.1.1.3 Signals are transmitted through the wires using specific hardware and software protocols (data packaging and signaling standards)
          1.1.1.1.4 Data moves through the physical network using these network protocols
      1.1.2 Network control
        1.1.2.1 Why network control is necessary
        1.1.2.2 Types of network control
          1.1.2.2.1 Hierarchical network (e.g., RTLL, CSAM, BRL/TRU)

1.1.2.2.1.1 One central host that controls the entire network

1.1.2.2.1.2 One host (system) within the network controls all data flow across the network

1.1.2.2.1.3 Requires adapter cards

1.1.2.2.2 Peer-to-peer network (TCP/IP, BDL, ZAQ201, ZPPN)

1.1.2.2.2.1 All the hosts in the network are equal (peers to each other) and equally control the network

1.1.2.2.2.2 No central controlling host required; each peer has its own network control program

1.1.2.2.2.3 Network control program must be running in each peer

1.1.2.2.2.4 SS/6000Z SPs are peer-to-peer

1.1.2.2.2.5 Requires adapter cards

1.1.2.2.3 Net-centric network (e.g., GGL, frame relay)

1.1.2.2.3.1 Does not require a host

1.1.2.2.3.2 No network operating system

1.1.2.2.3.3 Any host can be attached to this type of network

1.1.2.2.3.4 Requires some kind of box to attach to the network (e.g., 9125, router)

1.1.3 Network cabling [how to recognize cable type and connector]

1.1.3.1 Why you need to know about network cables

1.1.3.1.1 Each topology specifies valid cable types

1.1.3.1.2 To check the physical integrity of the cable and connector

1.1.3.2 Types of network cables

1.1.3.2.1 Type 1

1.1.3.2.1.1 Best wire but bulky and expensive

1.1.3.2.1.2 Black box connector (like the old token ring)

1.1.3.2.2 Type 5 (STP: Shielded Twisted Pair)

1.1.3.2.2.1 Next best wire but fairly expensive

1.1.3.2.2.2 RJ-45 connector

1.1.3.2.3 UTP: Unshielded twisted pair

1.1.3.2.3.1 Cheap but susceptible to noise

1.1.3.2.3.2 RJ-45 connector

1.1.3.2.4 Coax

    1.1.3.2.4.1 Strong and shielded but uncommon (used mainly for thin net)

    1.1.3.2.4.2 Requires termination

        1.1.3.2.4.2.1 Termination requires 50 Ohm terminators

    1.1.3.2.4.3 BNC

1.1.3.2.5 Fiber

[analysis continues from here—see appendix B for a more complete example]

Analyzing Attitudinal Objectives

To analyze attitudinal objectives, identify the indicator behaviors that demonstrate acquisition of the attitude and determine what factors will influence those indicator behaviors. The end result is a concise definition of the attitude that includes a list of agreed-upon indicator behaviors and a list of factors that influence those indicator behaviors.

Indicator behaviors are the outward, overt behaviors that an appointed group of subject matter experts (SMEs) agree will demonstrate that a person possesses a given attitude. Indicator behaviors are well defined if each SME can affirmatively answer the question, "If a person manifests these behaviors, will you agree that he or she possess the desired attitude?"

Consider the attitudinal objective, "Value the opinions of others on the team."

What indicator behaviors might demonstrate that a person possesses this attitude, and what factors influence those behaviors?

Here is one possible answer:

Objective: "Value the Opinions of Others on the Team."

Indicator Behaviors

- gives everyone equal opportunity to speak out and contribute to the conversation
- urges those who may be shy or reluctant to speak out and contribute
- keeps those who are overbearing or too outspoken from dominating the team
- defends weaker team members when others make fun of or make light of their comments
- treats comments from every team member with the same respect and dignity
- expresses appreciation to team members when they contribute opinions or ideas
- gives equal consideration to each idea, regardless of who it is from
- monitors his or her own speaking time and refrains from dominating the conversation

Factors That Influence These Indicator Behaviors

- hearing success stories about truly great ideas, inventions, or solutions that came from "weaker," less respected, or less outspoken team members
- understanding how creativity can be sparked and triggered by the comments of others
- understanding how being looked down upon or neglected on a team can lead to lack of contribution, resentment, and motivational problems
- understanding how each person seeing a different aspect of a problem can lead to better solutions
- being told that the indicator behaviors listed previously are expected behaviors of all employees and will be enforced
- participating in exercises that demonstrate any of these ideas
- rewarding team members when they manifest the indicator behaviors

---

The factors that influence the indicator behaviors might themselves need to be further analyzed using task analysis (for skills) or content analysis (for knowledge). These are assumed prerequisite skills to this book. If you do not know how to perform these techniques, see chapters 8 through 10 in my companion book, *Instructional Design—Step by Step: Nine Easy Steps for Designing Lean, Effective, and Motivational Instruction*. Bloomington, IN: iUniverse, 2013.

What Is the Final Output of Completing the Instructional Analysis to Determine All Enabling Content?

The final output of the first step in the development process is a collection of all of the enabling content that resulted from an analysis of each objective. More specifically:

- For skill or procedural objectives, the output is a collection of detailed step-by-step procedures and the detailed enabling information for the individual steps of those procedures.
- For attitudinal objectives, the output is the definition of the attitude, a list of indicator behaviors, and a list of factors that influence those indicator behaviors.
- For knowledge objectives, the output is the individual chunks of enabling information.

The output of this step is used as the input for the next step in the instructional development process: Classify information into its type and create corresponding instructional presentations.

Chapter Summary—Performing an Analysis of the Objectives to Determine All Enabling Content

This chapter discussed how to perform an analysis of the objectives to determine all of the enabling content that is required for a lesson or topic. This is the first step in the instructional development process.

You should now be able to

- describe the two inputs that are needed to complete the instructional analysis during instructional development,
- define and describe the SKA taxonomy at the level of a review,
- classify objectives using the SKA taxonomy,
- choose appropriate analysis techniques for each type of instructional objective,
- describe how to analyze skill objectives,
- describe how to analyze knowledge objectives,
- describe how to analyze attitudinal objectives, and
- describe the final output of identifying all enabling content.

Check Your Understanding

1. **What are the two inputs that are needed to complete the instructional analysis for a topic or lesson during instructional development? (Select all that apply.)**

   A. The objectives for the topic

   B. The topic exercises

   C. The topic introductions and summaries

   D. The requirements gathering template

   E. The combined instructional and content analysis that were performed for this particular lesson or topic during the design phase

   F. The sequence of events for the topic

2. **True or false? The SKA taxonomy classifies all learning into one of three types: Skills, Knowledge, and Aptitudes.**

3. **Classify each of the following objectives into a skill, knowledge, or attitude objective:**

   A. Actively seek new opportunities to sell e-business on demand.

   B. State the definition of a computer bus.

   C. Spell check a document.

   D. Determine the least common denominator of three fractions.

   E. Decide which sales strategy to take for a given client.

   F. Describe the major components of the XYZ storage subsystem.

   G. Choose to participate in the company 401K savings program.

4. **True or false? Skill objectives are analyzed using content analysis, knowledge objectives are analyzed using task and content analysis, and attitudinal objectives are analyzed by using indicator behavior analysis.**

5. **True or false? Skill objectives are analyzed by first using task analysis to drill the task down to a detailed step-by-step level and then using content analysis to identify the enabling content for each step.**

6. **True or false? The end result of analyzing a knowledge objective is a hierarchy of information with the lowest-level and most detailed information at the bottom of the hierarchy.**

7. **True or false? To analyze attitudinal objectives, assemble a group of experts and ask them to agree upon a definition of the attitude and the list of indicator behaviors; then, have them create a list of the factors that influence those indicator behaviors.**

8. **What is the final output of the first step in the development process—completing the instructional analysis to determine all enabling content? (Select all that apply.)**

   A. For knowledge objectives, the individual chunks of enabling information

   B. For all types of objectives, a list of instructional events for the topic

   C. A determination of the instructional delivery system to be used for that topic

D. For skill or procedural objectives, a collection of detailed step-by-step procedures and the detailed enabling information for the individual steps of those procedures

E. For attitudinal objectives, the definition of the attitude, a list of indicator behaviors, and a list of factors that influence those indicator behaviors

F. The sequence of objectives for the topic

Answers

1. A and E
2. False. The SKA taxonomy classifies all learning into one of three types: Skills, Knowledge, and *Attitudes*.
3. Objective A is choosing to perform an indicator action for an attitude. Objective B is demonstrating knowledge of a concept and is therefore a knowledge objective. Objective C is a procedure, which makes it a skill objective. Objective D is also a procedure, but one that is performed mentally or on paper, and is therefore a skill objective. Objective E is a procedure for making a decision and is therefore a skill objective. Objective F is demonstrating knowledge of a structure and is therefore a knowledge objective. Objective G is choosing to perform an indicator action for an attitude.
4. False. Skill objectives are analyzed using task and content analysis, knowledge objectives are analyzed using content analysis, and attitudinal objectives are analyzed by using indicator behavior analysis.
5. True
6. True
7. True
8. A, D, and E

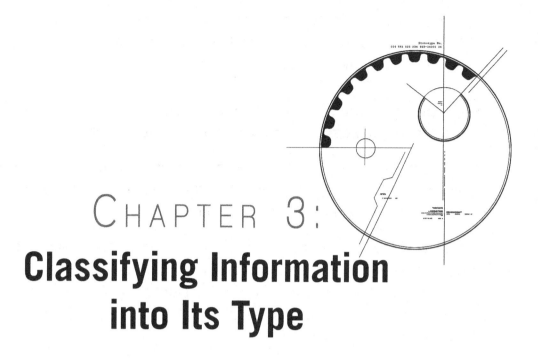

CHAPTER 3:
Classifying Information into Its Type

This chapter discusses how to classify information into its type. This task is part of the second step in the instructional development process.

Where We Are At in the Instructional Development Process

This chapter discusses part of step 2 in the instructional development process: how to classify information into its type and create corresponding instructional presentations. Other chapters in this part 1 discuss how to create corresponding instructional presentations for the seven types of information.

1. Analyze the objectives to determine all enabling content.
2. **Classify information into its type and create corresponding instructional presentations.**
3. Create the remaining instructional events and finalize the topic.

4. Create scripts (for technology-based training).

5. Perform a quality check on the training materials.

6. Pilot and revise all course materials.

Overview of How to Classify Information into Its Type and Create Corresponding Instructional Presentations

The output of the first step in the instructional development process is the individual chunks of enabling information that were identified in your instructional analysis and your analysis of each objective.

In step 2 of the instructional development process, you take this output and classify each piece of enabling information into its type using Robert Horn's taxonomy. You then design and create instructional presentations that employ research-based instructional strategies that most effectively teach information of that type.

Creating instructional presentations that present information based on its type is one of the key principles of instructional development. Following this principle will maximize the instructional effectiveness of your presentations because these strategies are designed to support the cognitive processing of each type of information. When content is taught some other way, learning might or might not be assured.

Step 2 in the instructional development process is typically the largest and most time consuming step in the development process because this is where you actually design and write the detailed training content for the topic.

A More Detailed Review of Robert Horn's Seven Information Types

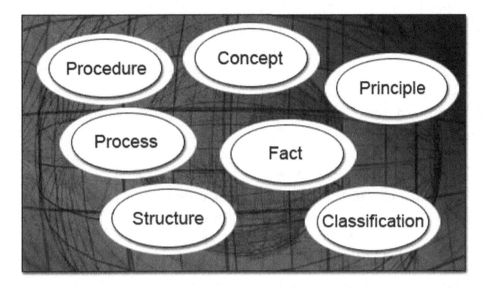

Figure 3. Robert Horn's seven types of information

In part 1, "Understanding How Humans Learn," in my companion book, *Instructional Design—Step by Step: Nine Easy Steps for Designing Lean, Effective, and Motivational Instruction*, you learned that you can classify all information into one of seven different types using Robert Horn's taxonomy. Because you will be using this taxonomy extensively in instructional development, you should become very familiar with it.

Review of Robert Horn's seven types of information

Procedure

Definition: A step-by-step method for achieving a specified outcome

Characteristics of procedures

- begins with a starting state and a set of inputs
- ends with the specified outcome
- tells the student how to do something
- written from the perspective of the student

Examples of procedures

- How to change a flat tire on a car
- How to create a header in a document
- How to replace the toner in the XYZ copier

Process

Definition: A description of how something functions or works or how things change over time

Characteristics of processes

- typically composed of major phases, stages, or events
- describes how things evolve as they go from one state to the next
- does not tell you how to produce the result
- written for understanding, not to perform

Examples of processes

- how glass is made
- how a bill becomes law
- how data is transmitted over the Internet
- how SSL encryption works
- what happens when **Enter** is pressed

Concept

Definition: Categories, groups, or classes of objects or ideas that all share certain similar attributes and are given a common label, even though they differ in some way.

Characteristics of concepts

- has a label, a definition, and a description of the common (or critical) attributes
- must have more than one member in the class (the set that includes all instances for that concept)

Examples of concepts

- chair
- token ring network
- e-business on demand

- context-sensitive menus
- an object (in object-oriented programming)

Principle

Definition: A principle either:

- tells a person what should or should not be done in various circumstances, or
- describes causal or logical relationships, such as what can be concluded in light of the evidence

Characteristics of principles

- typically describes policies, rules, heuristics, guidelines, relationships among classes of objects, warnings, requirements for certain conditions to be true, generalizations, and cause-and-effect relationships

Examples of principles

- Ohm's law.
- Client rapport improves sales.
- Increasing throughput requires more memory or CPU cycles.
- $E = mc^2$.
- When cooking, never add water to hot oil.

Fact

Definition: Simple assertion or statement that is assumed to be true

- stands on its own
- does not represent classes of objects or ideas as do concepts
- can be product specifications, dates when events occurred, proper names, names of parts, symbols used to represent things, and so forth

Examples of facts

- Temperature of the sun.
- Speed of a computer bus.
- New Year's Day is January 1.
- Maximum system memory.
- Water is made up of two hydrogen atoms and one oxygen atom.
- Press F9 to invoke spell check.

Structure

Definition: An object, physical or logical, that can be divided into component parts

- typically involves things that you can draw, diagram, represent, or photograph
- tells the student what something looks like and what its parts are

Examples of structures

- an organization chart
- an exploded view of a bicycle
- the grammatical structure of a sentence
- the parts of the main user interface for XYZ software
- a syntax diagram for a command

Classification

Definition: The assignment of specific items into two or more categories using some kind of sorting criteria

- Typically include words such as "types of," "kinds of," "sorts of," and "aspects of"
- Differ from facts because their purpose is to show how things are classified, not to state how things are

Examples of classifications

- types of loans
- the five types of editing functions
- the periodic table
- categories of error codes
- classification of animal life

How to Classify Information into Its Type

To classify information into its type:

1. Study the definitions and examples given previously for each information type.
2. Determine the *purpose* for presenting the information to the student.

For example, if students need to understand:

- how customer orders are received and processed, use a process.
- how to receive and process customer orders, use a procedure.
- which department handles which kind of complaint, use a classification.
- the client's business organization chart, use a structure.
- what e-commerce is, use a concept.
- who must sign off on the sales order, use a fact—unless, that is, certain rules or policies must be followed to determine who must sign off on the order, in which case use a principle.

Example of how the enabling content for an objective was classified into one of Horn's seven information types

Objective: Insert graphics files of all types into a Microsoft Word document

Enabling skills and content

- Use the copy and paste user interface function of Microsoft Office. [This is a procedure, but it is an assumed prerequisite skill for this course; therefore, it will *not* be taught.]
- What are graphics files? [This is a concept.]
- What are the various types of graphics files and their extensions? [This involves teaching a classification, two concepts, and related facts.]
- What is a frame? [This is a concept.]
- How to use frames. [This is a procedure.]
- Rules for frames. [This is a principle; related facts will be taught as part of the principle's definition.]
- How to insert a graphic file into a document. [This is a procedure.]
- What is clip art? [This is a concept.]
- How to insert clip art into a document. [This is a procedure.]

Example of Creating an Information Presentation Based on Its Type

Consider the concept, "What is a procedure?"

What would *you* do to teach this concept?

An instructionally sound strategy for teaching the concept, "What is a procedure?"

Provide a verbal definition of the concept

- "A procedure is a step-by-step method for achieving a specified outcome. It begins with a starting condition and a set of ..."

Discuss the concept's critical attributes

- Discuss the following critical attributes of the concept of a procedure: action steps, decision steps, starting and ending conditions, starting inputs, steps require action (mental or physical), and is written from a performer's point of view.

Present examples and non-examples of the concept with explanations of the reasons for their classifications

- "The following are examples of procedures ..."
- "The following are *not* examples of procedures for the reasons given ..."

Provide students the opportunity to practice classifying examples and non-examples of the concept

- "Classify the following descriptions as procedures or non-procedures ..."

Here are some additional resources for learning about Robert Horn's Information Mapping methodology:

- Web site: http://www.infomap.com
- *Mapping Hypertext: The Analysis, Organization, and Display of Knowledge for the Next Generation of On-Line Text and Graphics*, Robert E. Horn, Information Mapping, 1990, ISBN 0-96-255650-5. This book has two pages that describe the various types of information.

Chapter Summary—Classifying Information into Its Type

This chapter discussed how to classify information into its type. This task is part of the second step in the instructional development process.

You should now be able to

- give an overview of how to classify information into its type and how to create corresponding instructional presentations,
- define, describe, and provide examples of each of Robert Horn's seven types of information,
- describe in detail how to classify information into its type, and
- give an example of how information should be taught, based on its type.

Check Your Understanding

1. **True or false? Creating instructional segments that present information based on its type is one of the key principles of instructional development because doing so facilitates the cognitive processing of the information.**

2. **Match each type of information from Horn's taxonomy in the left-hand list with their definitions in the right-hand list.**

Procedure	A. A description of how something functions or works or how things change over time.
Process	B. Tells a person what should or should not be done in various circumstances, or describes causal or logical relationships, such as what can be concluded in light of the evidence.
Concept	C. Simple assertion or statement that is assumed to be true.
Principle	D. An object, physical or logical, that can be divided into component parts.
Fact	E. A step-by-step method for achieving a specified outcome.
Structure	F. The assignment of specific items into two or more categories using some kind of sorting criteria.
Classification	G. Categories, groups, or classes of objects or ideas that all share certain similar attributes and are given a common label, even though they differ in some way.

3. **In determining how to classify a piece of information into its type, what is the key thing you should consider?**
    A. How important the information is to the objectives
    B. Whether it can be further broken down into smaller components
    C. How complex the information is
    D. How the information relates to other information
    E. The purpose for presenting this information to the student

4. **Classify the following information into its type:**
    A. What is a bank?
    B. How to spell check a document
    C. How data moves from the web server to the enterprise storage server
    D. The parts of a nuclear power plant core containment building
    E. The types of Monarch butterflies
    F. The date that the World Wide Web was invented
    G. Travel expense guidelines

Answers

1. True
2. E, A, G, B, C, D, and F
3. E
4. A, concept; B, procedure; C, process; D, structure; E, classification; F, fact; and G, principle

CHAPTER 4:
Teaching Procedures

This chapter discusses how to teach procedures, one of the seven types of information. Teaching procedures is part of the second step in the instructional development process.

Where We Are At in the Instructional Development Process

This chapter is part of step 2 in the instructional development process: how to classify information into its type and create corresponding instructional presentations. It discusses how to create instructional presentations for one of the seven types of information—procedures. Subsequent chapters in part 1 discuss how to create instructional presentations for the other six types of information.

1.   Analyze the objectives to determine all enabling content.

2.   Classify information into its type and create corresponding instructional presentations.

3. Create the remaining instructional events and finalize the topic.

4. Create scripts (for technology-based training).

5. Perform a quality check on the training materials.

6. Pilot and revise all course materials.

Review of Procedures

A *procedure* is a step-by-step method for achieving a specified outcome. It begins with a starting condition and a set of inputs and ends with a recognizable outcome. Each step of a procedure is either an action step or a decision step, or a combination of the two.

Action steps ask the performer to take some kind of action, such as "Click the delete key," or "Attach the bolt." Decision steps ask the performer to answer a question, make a decision, or choose an alternative depending on real-life conditions, such as "Click one of the following options," "Choose which file format to use," and "Is the customer's credit score above 400?"

Procedures tell the student *how to do* something—the specific actions to take, decisions to make, and the order to execute them—and are written from the perspective of the *performer* of the actions.

Examples of procedures include "How to change a flat tire on a car," "How to create a header in a document," How to decide how much money to reinvest in the company," and "How to replace the toner in the XYZ copier."

Teaching Procedures

Because much training is devoted to teaching students procedures (skills), we will discuss how to teach procedures in some detail in this chapter.

Procedures are made up of a series of steps (action and decision steps), a title, a starting condition, a terminating condition, and the enabling content required for each step. To teach a procedure, use step-by-step instructions as the overall organizing framework for presenting the procedure, unless a special circumstance exists that calls for an exception.

Use the following guidelines in designing and creating your instructional presentations:

1. Write a descriptive title.

Write the title so that it is clear that this is a procedure, and what the procedure is about. Make the title accurate, clear, and complete. Two common forms for writing procedure titles are:

- "How to ..." For example, "How to Sell a Widget" or "How to Operate the 2080 Turret"
- "XYZing ..." where "XYZing" is a gerund. For example, "Selling a Widget" or "Operating the 2080 Turret"

2. Provide numbered steps.

Organize the procedure into a series of numbered step-by-step actions that a person must perform to carry out the procedure. Numbers strongly imply an order or sequence and help the student track their place in the procedure.

3. Describe what the procedure will do.

Provide a more detailed overview of what the procedure does than just what is conveyed by the title of the procedure. This is usually a sentence or a paragraph. If the procedure can accomplish multiple tasks, be sure to describe each one. Those performing the procedure should be able to read this description and tell if this is the procedure that they are looking for.

4. State the starting conditions that should be present before the procedure is performed.

If the *starting conditions*—the specific situations in which the procedure is appropriately applied—are not obvious, describe them in enough detail so that the performer will know if these conditions are met. Teach any enabling content that is necessary for the performer to recognize these conditions and decide on whether these conditions have been met.

5. Create bite-sized steps.

Break the procedure into manageable steps consisting of one or two actions per step. Multiple actions *within a step* tend to get lost in the instructional text. If you must include several actions in a single step—rather than breaking them out into multiple steps—format them in a bulleted list, column, or table.

6. For action steps, tell performers both what to do and what will happen as a result of taking that action.

In addition, distinguish action text from text describing the results by

- using labels ("Action," "Result"),
- consistent positioning (action in the left column of a table, result in the right column),
- typographic distinctions, such as bold or italic text, and
- placing the result as a separate paragraph just after the action text.

Provide a consistent visual coding of action and result information to assist comprehension.

For example

1. Click the **delete** icon.
   The text is deleted and disappears from the page.
2. Click the drop-down button.
   The edit menu appears.

Explain what the performer should expect to see as a result of taking the action so that the performer can verify that the action did what it was intended to do.

7. For decision steps, tell performers how to make the decision.

For *decision steps*—steps that ask a question or that require different actions depending on real-life conditions—describe the procedure for making the decision in enough detail that the performer can arrive at the correct decision or option. This is a critical part of the enabling information that is often left out by trainers, which causes performers to stumble or fail at this point in the procedure. In fact, how to make the decision might be complicated enough to require that this "How to decide …" procedure be taught as well.

Next, for each condition or decision outcome, describe where the performer should go to find the next step in the procedure, if it is not obvious. For example, "If yes, go to step 10; if no, go to step 12."

8. Describe the terminating conditions.

Tell the performer how to know when the procedure is complete and what the final output should be. In other words, tell the performer how to know if the procedure was successful.

9. Teach enabling content within each step.

For each step, teach any enabling information that is required to carry out that step's action or make that step's decision. Include only enabling information that is relevant to that step. Teaching enabling content right where it is needed makes it easy to remember and apply. Moreover, it will be viewed as highly relevant to the training.

If enabling information is extensive, complex, or common across many steps, consider teaching it as a whole upfront before presenting the actual steps of the procedure. This is especially true if the enabling information can be better understood as an integrated, well-organized body of information rather than as a collection of many pieces of seemingly disjointed information.

10. Layer large or complex procedures.

If the procedure is large or complex, consider layering the detail of the steps of the procedure. In other words, present a high-level step-by-step description of the procedure first as an organizing framework or overview; then teach the detailed subprocedures related to each major step afterward using the framework to maintain context.

11. Use an understandable, consistent layout to facilitate comprehension and ease of use.

Organize the layout of the steps of the procedure by using numbered steps, tables, labelled columns, or some other organizing technique. Clearly distinguish the different kinds of information that appear, such as step numbers, instructions, feedback, enabling information, warnings, and cautions by using typography, labels, and positioning techniques. Be consistent in following your chosen style and layout.

12. Give examples of performing difficult, complex, or potentially confusing steps.

If the action for a particular step is particularly difficult or complex, provide an example within the step that shows how to perform the action for that step. An example is often worth a thousand words.

13. Provide a demonstration of the procedure.

Provide a demonstration of the procedure, especially if it is challenging, complex, or full of pitfalls. A demonstration is a powerful instructional technique.

14. Speak to the student directly.

Write procedural instructions in active, second-person imperative voice as if a master performer was telling the student how to carry out the procedure.

15. Provide supportive graphics where needed.

Provide supportive graphics if steps require any of the following:

- psychomotor skills, such as hand-eye, body, or muscular coordination (this situation may require a series of graphics or a multimedia presentation)
- the identification of the item to be acted upon among a complex visual stimulus
- a view of an object from a particular visual angle or orientation

Some procedural presentation layouts use a column in a table to visually highlight the object to be acted upon or the result of taking the action.

16. If a decision step is complex, consider using a decision table.

A decision table shows the conditions that vary as headers along the top and the action to take based on a specific combination of conditions in the rightmost column. The performer reads the table from left to right. In the following table, for example, if the error indicator LED is yellow and the voltage is less than .5, than the performer should flip DIP switch 2 and test again:

If the error indicator LED is	And the voltage is	Then
Green	Less than .5	Increase the voltage adjustment by .1 volts and test again.
	Greater than or equal to .5	The unit is working properly. Continue to Step 5.
Yellow	Less than .5	Flip DIP switch 2 and test again.
	Great than or equal to .5	Flip DIP switch 5 and test again.
Red	—	Replace the unit and test again.

Note: A dash in a cell means that this condition is simply ignored for this combination of logic. For example, in the table above, if the error indicator LED is red, then the performer should replace the unit and test again, regardless of the voltage reading.

17. Consider using tables to organize steps.

A table is one technique for organizing the steps of a procedure. Consider the following two examples:

How to Check the Spelling of a Document

Step	Action
1	Click the spelling icon: [ABC]\s

The spelling dialog box is displayed. |
| 2 | ... |

How to Check the Spelling of a Document

Step	Action	Result
1	Click the spelling icon: [ABC]\s	The spelling dialog box is displayed.
2	...	...

18. Consider using flowcharts to organize steps.

Flowcharts are often used when there is a limited amount of branching in a procedure and where the visual flow is an important part of what students or performers need to understand.

The following figure is an example of a flowchart:

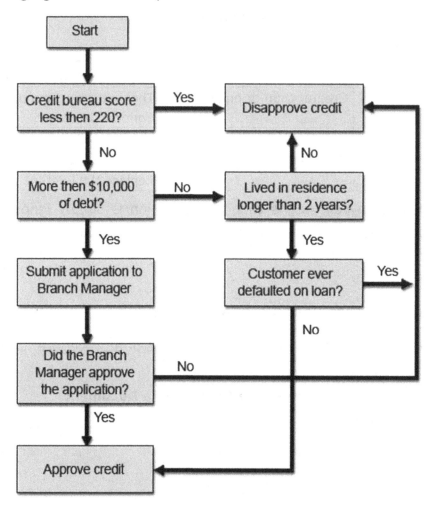

Figure 4. Example of a flowchart: How to determine if customer credit should be approved

19. Begin each action step with a verb.

A procedure is a step-by-step series of imperative instructions. Therefore, begin each action step with a verb. For action steps, use the imperative form of the verb: "Click enter" or "Slide the case onto the unit."

Exceptions to this rule exist when you want to emphasize a qualifying condition for how the action should be taken for safety, quality control, or other special reasons; for example, "Using the CPU mounting tool, install the CPU in the rack" or "Without touching the grounding lug, position the motherboard in the chassis."

20. Begin each decision step with a lead in or list of choices.

For decision steps, either provide a lead in for a list of choices, as in "Choose one of the following ..." or "Determine which of the following applies," or provide the condition at the beginning of the sentence, as in, "If the package label is red, place it in the rework bin; if the package label is green, place it on the shipping rack."

21. Be consistent across the entire procedure.

Use consistent layout, phrasing, grammatical structures, visual encoding, and style across the entire procedure. Consistency leads to faster comprehension.

Chapter Summary –Teaching Procedures

This chapter discussed how to teach procedures, one of the seven types of information. Teaching procedures is part of the second step in the instructional development process.

You should now be able to

- define and describe procedures and give several examples of them;
- describe how to write descriptive procedure titles and why numbering steps is important;
- describe how to create an overview of the procedure, state the starting conditions, and create bite-sized steps;
- do the following in teaching procedures:
  - for action steps, describe why it is important to tell performers both what to do and what will happen as a result of taking that action;
  - for decision steps, explain why it is important to tell performers how to make the decision;
  - describe why you should explain the terminating conditions;
  - describe how to teach enabling content within each step and why it is important;
  - describe how to layer large or complex procedures;
  - describe why it is important to use a good, consistent layout;
  - describe why it is important to provide examples of performing difficult, complex, or potentially confusing steps;
  - describe why it is important to provide a demonstration of the procedure;
  - describe how to speak to the student directly;
  - describe how to provide supportive graphics where needed;
  - for complex decision steps, describe when to consider using a decision table;
  - describe when to consider using tables to organize steps;
  - describe when to consider using flowcharts to organize steps;
  - describe how to begin each action step with a verb;
  - describe how to begin each decision step with a lead in or list of choices; and

- describe why it is important to be consistent across the entire procedure.

Check Your Understanding

1. **True or false? A process is a step-by-step method for achieving a specified outcome.**

2. **For each title, indicate if it is the title for a procedure or for something else:**
   A. How to Remove Wallpaper from Interior Walls
   B. How Potholes Are Fixed in Asphalt Roads
   C. Boating Safety Rules
   D. Fixing a Flat Tire on a Bicycle
   E. How Trees Are Made into Paper
   F. How to Decide if You Should Invest in the Stock Market
   G. How Tax Forms Are Processed
   H. How to Complete Your Tax Forms
   I. Growing Huge Vegetables in Your Garden

3. **True or false? In teaching procedures, you should avoid including a large number of actions in a single step.**

4. **In teaching action steps in procedures, you should: (Select all that apply.)**
   A. Tell performers what to do.
   B. Tell performers how to make decisions.
   C. Describe the terminating conditions.
   D. Tell performers what will happen as a result of taking the action.
   E. Use consistent labeling, positioning, or typography to help performers distinguish different types of information.
   F. Always place the action before the conditions.

5. **True or false? When teaching decision steps in procedures, you should explain in detail *how* to make the decision unless you are absolutely sure that your target audience already knows how to make that decision.**

6. **True or false? In teaching the steps of a procedure, you must also teach the enabling content for that step, preferably at that very point in the instruction or, for more complex enabling content that is repeatedly used across several steps, in an upfront section or topic of its own.**

7. **In teaching procedures, provide a _____ of the procedure, especially if it is challenging, complex, or full of pitfalls.**

8. **In teaching procedures, you should consider providing supportive graphics if step actions require: (Select all that apply.)**
   A. A mental mathematical calculation.
   B. The simple press of a key on the keyboard.
   C. A view of an object from a particular visual angle or orientation.
   D. Psychomotor skills, such as hand-eye, body, or muscular coordination.
   E. The performer to reflect on a question.
   F. The identification of the item to be acted upon among complex visual stimulus.

9. **True or false? A decision table is read from left to right and typically shows the conditions that vary as headers along the top and the action to take based on a certain combination of conditions in the rightmost column.**

10. **True or false? In teaching procedures, step-action tables or step-action-result tables are commonly used to organize the information.**

11. **True or false? In teaching procedures, flowcharts are often used when there is a limited amount of branching in a procedure and where the visual flow is an important part of what students need to understand.**

12. **In teaching procedures, instructions that begin with "Choose one of the following ..." "Determine which of the following applies," or "If the package label is red, place it in the rework bin" indicate that this step is a _____ step.**

Answers

1. False. A *procedure* is a step-by-step method for achieving a specified outcome.
2. A, title for a procedure; B, title for something else; C, title for something else; D, title for a procedure; E, title for something else; F, title for a procedure; G, title for something else; H, title for a procedure, and I, title for a procedure.
3. True
4. A, D, and E
5. True. Be careful that you do not casually decide that your target audience can already make this decision. A lack of decision support for decision steps within procedures is a major cause of why students cannot learn to perform procedures successfully. To provide this support, you might even have to teach a sophisticated procedure on how to make that decision in addition to the procedure that you are teaching.
6. True
7. The correct answer is "demonstration."
8. C, D, and F
9. True
10. True
11. True
12. The correct answer is "decision."

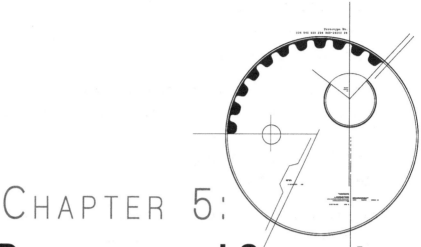

CHAPTER 5:

Teaching Processes and Concepts

This chapter discusses how to teach processes and concepts—two of the seven types of information.

Where We Are At in the Instructional Development Process

This chapter is part of step 2 in the development process—it discusses how to create instructional presentations for two of the seven types of information: processes and concepts. Other chapters in Part 1 discuss how to create instructional presentations for the other five types of information.

1. Perform an analysis of the objectives to determine all enabling content.
2. **Classify information into its type and create corresponding instructional presentations.**
3. Create the remaining instructional events and finalize the topic.
4. Create scripts (for technology-based training).
5. Perform a quality check on the training materials.

6. Pilot and revise all course materials.

Review of Processes

The next type of information that we will discuss is processes. A *process* describes how something functions or works or how things change over time. It is made up of the major phases, stages, or events that describe how entity A evolves to become or produce entity B and how things transition from one stage or phase to the next.

For example, a process documents how event A leads to, triggers, or sets the stage for event B which leads to event C and so on until a final result or state is achieved.

Examples of processes include:

- "how a weather forecast is made"
- "how an http:// request is processed by a web server"

Contrast these examples to the following examples of things that are *not* processes (they are procedures):

- "how to make a weather forecast"
- "how to program a web server to process http:// requests"

How Processes Differ from Procedures

Processes do not tell you *how* to produce the final result like a procedure does; rather, they tell you what happens over time that leads to the final outcome.

The process of how glass is manufactured is a high-level description of the sequence of overall events that occur in making glass.

Here is an example of a process for making glass:

1. The raw ingredients for glass are ordered (sand, soda, and lime).
2. These ingredients are shipped to and received by the glass manufacturer and placed in temporary storage bins.

3. The ingredients are then mixed in proper proportion and heated and melted in a furnace.
4. The molten glass is then poured into a machine that creates continuous sheets of soft, hot glass.
5. These sheets then pass through a water bath to cool the glass down.
6. The glass is then cut, packaged, and shipped to the customer.

Compare this example to the *procedure* for how glass is made, which consists of dozens of company operating manuals containing the detailed step-by-step instructions for ordering materials, mixing ingredients, running furnaces, operating equipment, checking chemical compositions, and so forth. Processes are written for understanding and are written from an observer's perspective. Procedures are written to be followed and carried out by a performer.

The following table provides examples of processes and their procedural counterparts:

Process	Procedure
How glass is manufactured	How to manufacture glass
How things move through the supply chain of a company	How to order and move things through the supply chain of company XYZ
How a sales order is processed	How to process a sales order
How data moves through the e-commerce server to the enterprise storage systems databases	How to program the code that moves data through an e-commerce server to enterprise storage systems databases
How an http:// request is received and processed on a web server	How to program a web server to process http:// requests
How a water utility runs its business	How to run a water utility
How customer complaints are handled	How to handle a customer complaint
What happens when customers default on a loan	How to handle a customer's loan when it is in default
What happens when the OP_ERROR command is issued	How to issue the OP_ERROR command

Notice that processes always describe how things change or proceed over time, not the specific actions or steps a person must take to *make* or *cause* a particular result to occur.

Notice also that while processes are often verbally described by passive sentences that begin with the word "How ..." they *never* begin with the two words "How to ..." As an alternative to using passive voice in titles, processes can also be worded as "How [a third party does something]." For example, "How companies manufacture glass."

Teaching Processes

The main components of a process are the major *phases, stages,* or *events* that occur as things go from one state or condition to another over time. Make these major phases, stages, or events easily discernible to students. They serve as the overall organizing framework for the process. To teach processes, follow these additional guidelines:

1. Provide context, background, and overview information.

Provide context or background information for the process that describes why you are presenting this process, what the process is (in a sentence or two), what the starting state or condition is when the process begins, what the outputs or ending state of the process are, and any other information that is necessary to place the process in a proper framework or context.

2. For large or complex processes, break the process into phases or stages.

If the process is large or complex, consider layering the detailed discussions of each phase. Examples of large or complex processes are "How cars are manufactured" and "How an enterprise web server processes web requests." Break the process into nine or fewer stages. First present a high-level overview of the stages, events, or phases as an organizing framework or overview and then teach the detailed subprocesses related to each major phase using this framework to maintain context.

3. For small or simple processes, simply describe the sequence of events.

For simple or small processes, simply provide a verbal or textual narrative of the sequence of events for how things move or change from the start of the process to its end.

4. Describe the major stages, phases, or events.

Break the process into the major time intervals, phases, stages, or events that make up the process, label them appropriately, and check that they are in proper sequence. Make sure that it is clear what the time interval is or grouping of events are that each stage or phase covers.

If the process involves people and it is important for the instructional objectives to describe their role in the process, describe who does what with what in each stage. Describe each stage or event to the necessary level of detail to meet the lesson objective. Within the description, teach any concepts, facts, structures, procedures, processes, classifications, and principles that students need to understand—the enabling content for that stage or phase of the process. Do not describe the process in any more detail than is required to achieve the lesson or topic's objectives.

5. Take an observer's perspective.

In describing the stages, phases, or events of a process, use the third person, active voice: "First this occurs, then that occurs ..." For example:

1. Receiving accepts shipments of raw cloth and feeds them into assembly as needed.
2. Assembly cuts and assembles the garments and sends them on to quality control.
3. Quality control checks the garments, rejects any defective ones, and sends good ones on to shipping.
4. Shipping packages, invoices, and ships the product.

Sometimes a third-person, passive voice is used to place a particular emphasis on an object or to achieve a different perspective.

1. The raw cloth is received by shipping and fed into assembly.

2. The garments are then cut and assembled from the cloth and sent on to quality control.

3. The garments are checked by quality control for defects and either sent back to assembly for repair or sent on to shipping.

4. The garments are finally packaged, invoiced, and shipped.

Writing a process is somewhat like writing a mini-documentary of how something works or evolves over time from one state to another.

6. Use graphics to enhance understanding, as appropriate.

A graphical overview or illustration of the process can often facilitate the understanding and remembering of a process. Some of the critical elements of a process that need to be illustrated in the graphic are:

- The major phases of the process
- The direction of flow from one phase to the next, often depicted with arrows
- If the process is time based, an indication of the flow of time using arrows, a numbered sequence, or an explicit or implicit horizontal or vertical time axis.

If it is important to understand how a given object changes state through a process, consider showing a graphical "snapshot" of the state of the object at each major stage along with an indication of the triggers that transition the object from one state to another.

7. Consider using tables to organize and present a process.

Tables are not only useful for organizing and presenting procedures, but for organizing and presenting processes as well. Replace numbered steps with the numbered or labeled major phases of the process and replace action instructions with descriptions of the phases.

The following table shows an example of how to use a table to organize and present a process:

How Sales Orders Are Processed and Fulfilled

Phase	Who	Performs what
1. Order receipt	Telesales specialist	Receives email notification of a new pending sale from the Order Entry application Brings the order up on the Sales Order Entry application Assigns an invoice and customer ID Sends the order on to order qualification
2. Order qualification	Qualifying specialist	Qualifies the order and validates that the required information was submitted Validates payment capability Rejects and returns faulty orders
3. Order processing	Fulfillment specialist	Commits individual products to orders from stock Submits backorders for products out of stock Notifies the customer of the status of the order Creates shipping and packing instructions and sends them to shipping
4. Shipping	Shipping specialist	Picks and packages the items for an order Ships the order Invoices the customer and copies accounting
5. Accounting	Accounting specialist	Receives payment for orders and updates the books Sends out dunning notices Turns delinquent accounts over to the collection agency

8. Consider using flowcharts to organize and present a process.

Consider using a flowchart to depict the major events of a process if there is a limited amount of branching in the process and if the visual flow is an important part of what students or performers need to understand.

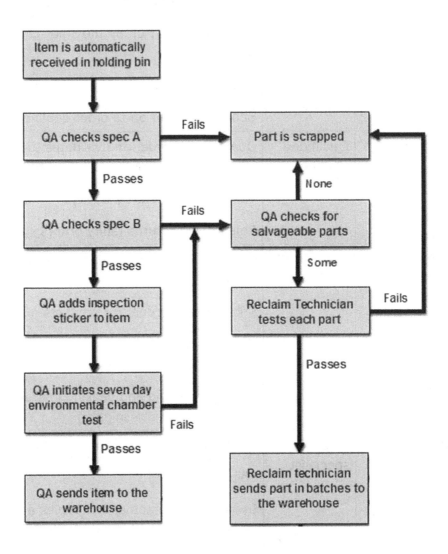

Figure 5. Example of using a flowchart to organize and present a process: How items are checked in Product Quality

9. Provide examples of the process.

Provide a specific example of how the process works. Examples are worth a thousand words. For example, if you are teaching the process for how a political bill is proposed, debated, and passed by the governing body, consider providing a specific example of how a previous bill was proposed, debated, and passed so that students can see how the process works in real life.

Review of Concepts

The next type of information that we will discuss is concepts.

Concepts are categories, groups, or classes of objects or ideas that all share similar attributes and are given a common label, even though they differ in some ways. For example, there are many different varieties of chairs, but they all share a core set of similar attributes.

To identify concepts, look for new jargon or terminology, classes of things or ideas that are given a common name, and any other ideas that have *defining characteristics*, *multiple members*, and a *common label*.

Examples of concepts include

- chair,
- bank,
- object-oriented programming,
- e-business,
- win-win negotiation,
- compound interest, and
- time.

Teaching Concepts

One key part of a concept is its definition. The definition for a concept should include the name of the concept—"chair"—and its defining attributes—"is used for sitting," "usually but does not always have four or more legs." The definition must be precisely written so that students can determine if a new object or idea belongs to the class of objects or ideas represented by the concept. For example, if a new object is not used for sitting, it is not a chair.

In teaching concepts, you must do more than just present a well-written definition of the concept. In most cases, you should also provide examples and non-examples of the concept along with explanations for why each example belongs or does not belong to the class of things represented by the concept. Students should then be required to practice classifying previously unencountered instances and non-instances of the concept. These techniques are further explained in the following guidelines.

1. Provide the label or name for the concept.

Provide and call out (emphasize) the official or accepted name for the concept. For example, "Definition of a widget," or "A widget is a ..."

2. Provide a definition that includes the required and variable critical attributes.

The *critical attributes* of a concept are the attributes that must always be present for something to be classified as an example of that concept. For example, for the concept of a chair, the critical attributes might be "a physical object" and "used for sitting." Describe the critical attributes of the concept with sufficient detail and clarity that the student can determine if a new thing, object, or idea is an instance of the concept—that it possesses all of the required and defining attributes of the concept.

The *variable attributes* of a concept are attributes that may or may not be present or that vary from instance to instance of the concept. For example, the variable attributes for the concept of a chair might be "number of legs," "chair back," and "height."

3. Clarify the concept's boundary.

The *concept boundary* distinguishes what is a member of the concept's class from what is not. It is clarified by writing excellent definitions and by providing representative examples and non-examples of the concept, including some that might easily be misclassified.

4. Provide a variety of examples.

Examples are instances of the concept. Always provide two or more examples of a concept. For concepts with variable attributes that might or might not be present or that are present in widely varying degrees or forms, provide several examples, each with different variable attributes.

For example, if one of the variable attributes of "motorized land vehicle" is "moves across the ground," provide as examples

- a car with four wheels,
- a truck with four or six wheels,
- a bus with 10 wheels,
- a tractor trailer with 18 wheels,
- an airfoil with no wheels,
- a snowmobile with a belt tread,
- a motorcycle with two wheels, and
- an army tank with steel-link treads.

Annotate your examples with explanations if it is not obvious to the reader how each example fulfills the critical and variable attributes of the concept's definition.

5. Provide a variety of non-examples.

Non-examples are things or ideas that are *not* instances of the concept. They do not fulfill one or more of the critical attributes of the concept. Well-chosen non-examples are just as important and powerful as well-chosen examples in helping students learn a concept. They further clarify and define the boundaries of the concept in students' minds and point out common errors in classification.

For example, non-examples of the concept "motorized land vehicle" might include

- a bicycle (no motor),

- a skateboard (no motor),
- a human-powered aircraft (no motor),
- a surfboard (no motor),
- a jet aircraft (flies in the air well above the ground), and
- a motorized paraglider (flies in the air well above the ground).

Annotate your non-examples with explanations that explain why each non-example fails to fulfill one or more of the critical attributes of the definition.

6. Provide *both* examples and non-examples.

Definitions of concepts can be abstract and difficult to understand. So how do you know when students understand a concept? Students understand a concept when they can correctly classify a variety of previously unencountered instances and non-instances of the concept. Students must learn to reject close-in non-examples that are similar to but different than genuine instances of the concept. To assist in this refinement, you must provide *both* obvious and non-obvious examples and non-examples and provide explanations that justify their classification.

7. Give special treatment to easy-to-misclassify examples and non-examples that appear on first glance to be members or non-members of the concept class.

Clear-cut examples and non-examples are those that clearly comply with or violate, respectively, one or more of the concept's critical attributes. On the other hand, *easy-to-misclassify examples and non-examples* are instances that appear on first glance to be examples or non-examples but in reality are just the opposite of what one might expect. For the concept of a mammal, easy-to-misclassify examples might be "a whale is a mammal" and "a bat is a mammal."

Provide easy-to-misclassify examples and non-examples if students are ever likely to encounter them or if they will help students achieve the level of understanding of the concept that is required by the lesson objective. Always provide detailed and thorough explanations for why they are or are not instances of the concept.

An example of the critical elements for teaching the concept of a mammal:

Definition: A *mammal* is an animal that

- is vertebrate (has a backbone),
- feeds its young on mother's milk,
- has hair at some time in its life,
- is warm-blooded, and
- has a larger, more developed brain than other animals.

Examples of mammals

- humans
- cats
- cows

Non-examples of mammals

- chickens
- oak trees
- trout
- bees

Easy to misclassify examples

- whales (they look like a big fish and have hair only before they are born)
- porpoises
- bats (most mammals do not fly)
- platypuses

Remember, well-chosen examples and non-examples are often worth a thousand instructional words.

8. Provide practice in classifying previously unencountered instances and non-instances.

Present students with previously unseen examples and non-examples of the concept and ask them to determine if they are instances of the concept and explain their reasons why. In this practice, start with simple, clear-cut examples and non-examples to build students' confidence and then move to more difficult to classify or easy-to-misclassify instances to refine students' accuracy in making fine discriminations. Have students practice classifying items with different variable attributes as well. As always, provide detailed feedback so students can improve their understanding of the concept's boundaries.

Providing students the opportunity to practice classifying new objects as instances or non-instances of the concept and receiving feedback on their judgments is critical in teaching concepts.

9. Provide analogies to clarify difficult or obscure concepts.

Analogies are excellent to use in teaching concepts that involve new, foreign, or difficult-to-understand definitions and critical attributes. Examples include using an inverted tree analogy to illustrate the concept of a computer file system, or using the analogy of a mail-sorting cabinet to illustrate the concept of computer memory as sequential locations for the storage of bytes of information.

Chapter Summary—Teaching Processes and Concepts

This chapter discussed how to teach processes and concepts—two of the seven types of information.

You should now be able to

- define and describe processes and give several examples of them,
- explain how processes differ from procedures,
- do the following in teaching processes:
  - describe what should be included in the context and background information for the process,
  - for large or complex processes, explain why it is important to break the process into phases or stages,
  - describe how to teach small or simple processes,
  - describe what to teach about the major stages, phases, or events,
  - explain how to take an observer's perspective,
  - describe how to use graphics to enhance understanding,
  - describe when you should consider using tables to organize and present a process and how the table should be structured,
  - describe when to consider using flowcharts to organize and present a process,
  - describe why it is important to provide examples of the process,
- define and describe concepts and give several examples of them,
- list the major instructional elements that you should include in teaching concepts,
- do the following in teaching concepts:
  - describe how to create a definition of a concept and use critical and variable attributes to define the boundary of the concept,
  - describe what types of examples to provide,
  - describe what types of non-examples to provide,
  - explain why it is important to include both examples and non-examples,
  - explain why it is important to give special attention to including easy-to-misclassify examples and non-examples that appear on first glance to be members or non-members of the concept class,

- explain why you should provide practice in classifying previously unencountered instances and non-instances, and
- explain how to use analogies to clarify difficult or obscure concepts.

Check Your Understanding

1. **True or false? A *process* describes how something functions or works or how things change over time.**

2. **True or false? Processes do not tell you *how* to produce the final result like a procedure does; rather, they tell you what happens over time that leads to the final outcome.**

3. **Classify each of the following statements into processes or procedures:**
   A. How to change a flat tire
   B. How mountains are formed
   C. Pruning rose bushes
   D. How the Internet works
   E. Getting stains out of shirts
   F. The lifecycle of water on planet earth
   G. How steel is made

4. **How should you teach large or complex processes?**
   A. Start with the first stage, event, or phase, teach all of the detailed information related to that stage, then go to the next stage, teach all of the detailed information related to that stage, and so forth.
   B. Begin with a demonstration of the process and then take whatever approach you think is most effective.
   C. First present a high-level overview of the stages, events, or phases as an organizing framework or overview and then teach the detailed subprocesses related to each major phase using this framework to maintain context.
   D. Bring in an expert to discuss or document the process.

5. **True or false? In teaching processes, if a process involves people and it is important to the instructional objectives that students**

describe the role or these people in the process, describe who does what in each stage.

6. **True or false? In teaching the stages, phases, or events of a process, take an observer's perspective by using the third person, active voice or the third person passive voice, as appropriate.**

7. **In teaching processes, what situations typically call for a graphical illustration? (Select all that apply.)**
    A. Defining concepts that are part of the enabling content for the process
    B. Showing the direction of flow from one phase to the next
    C. Overviewing the major phases of the process
    D. Describing the context for when the process occurs
    E. Teaching a process that is heavily tied to a time schedule

8. **How do tables that are used to present procedures differ from tables that are used to present processes?**
    A. They do not differ at all.
    B. The table is arranged in a horizontal format for process tables and a vertical format in procedure tables.
    C. The numbered steps in procedure tables are removed and the action instructions in procedure tables become the phase descriptions in process tables.
    D. The numbered steps in procedure tables are replaced with the numbered or labeled major phases of the process, and the action instructions in procedure tables are replaced with phase descriptions in process tables.

9. **True or false? Consider using a flowchart to depict the major events of a process if there is a limited amount of branching in the process and if the visual flow is an important part of what students or performers need to understand.**

10. **True or false? Classifications are categories, groups, or classes of objects or ideas that all share similar attributes and are given a common label, even though they differ in some ways.**

11. **To determine whether information is a concept, you should check to see if it has: (Select all that apply.)**
    A. Defining characteristics
    B. Agreement among SMEs that it is a concept
    C. Only a single member or instance
    D. Multiple members or instances
    E. A lengthy explanation
    F. A common label

12. **In teaching concepts, you should: (Select all that apply.)**
    A. Provide a definition of the concept that includes the name of the concept and the required and variable attributes.
    B. Provide well-chosen examples (instances) of the concept.
    C. Provide well-chosen non-examples (non-instances) of the concept.
    D. Provide and explain commonly misclassified examples and non-examples of the concept.
    E. Provide students the opportunity to classify previously unencountered instances and non-instances of the concept and receive feedback.

13. **True or false? In teaching concepts, clarify the boundary of the concept by providing several definitions of the concept from different subject matter experts or recognized authorities.**

14. **True or false? Well-chosen non-examples are just as important and powerful as well-chosen examples in helping students to learn a concept because they further clarify and define the boundaries of the concept in students' minds and point out common errors in classification.**

15. **If you were teaching the concept of a mammal, a whale would be:**
    A. An example of a fish that you should include in your training.
    B. A mainstream example of the concept.
    C. An easily misclassified non-example of the concept.
    D. An easily misclassified example of the concept.

E. An example that you would not want to include in your training so that students do not become confused.

16. **True or false? In teaching concepts, students' understanding of a concept can be determined by asking them to classify previously encountered instances (examples) of the concept.**

Answers

1. True
2. True
3. A, procedure; B, process; C, procedure; D, process; E, procedure; F, process; G, process. Statements A, C, and E all convey step-by-step tasks to be performed to accomplish a specific result. The other statements convey third-person descriptions for a process—for how things change or move from one state to another. Statement G, for example, would be a procedure if it stated, "How to make steel."
4. C
5. True
6. True
7. B, C, and E
8. D
9. True
10. False. *Concepts* are categories, groups, or classes of objects or ideas that all share similar attributes and are given a common label, even though they differ in some ways.
11. A, D, and F
12. A, B, C, D, and E.
13. False. In teaching concepts, you clarify the boundary of the concept by providing *representative examples and non-examples* of the concept, including some that might easily be misclassified.
14. True
15. D

16. False. You should ask them to classify previously *un*encountered instances of the concept. If you ask them to classify instances (examples) that they have already seen, they might have simply memorized the fact that the examples are instances of the concept instead of applying the criteria and making a determination according to that criteria.

CHAPTER 6:
Teaching Principles, Facts, Structures, and Classifications

This chapter discusses how to teach principles, facts, structures, and classifications—four of the seven types of information.

Where We Are At in the Instructional Development Process

This chapter is part of step 2 in the development process—it discusses how to create instructional presentations for four of the seven types of information: principles, facts, structures, and classifications. Other chapters in Part 1 discuss how to create instructional presentations for the other three types of information.

1. Perform an analysis of the objectives to determine all enabling content.
2. **Classify information into its type and create corresponding instructional presentations.**

3. Create the remaining instructional events and finalize the topic.
4. Create scripts (for technology-based training).
5. Perform a quality check on the training materials.
6. Pilot and revise all course materials.

Review of Principles

Another type of information is principles. To review, *principles* are either:

- *Behavioral principles*, which tell a person what should or should not be done in various circumstances.
- *General principles*, which describe causal or logical relationships, such as what can be concluded in light of the evidence.

Principles typically describe policies, rules, heuristics, guidelines, relationships between classes of objects, warnings, requirements for certain conditions to be true, generalizations, or criteria that should be applied or that lead to a certain conclusion.

Statements that begin with "Do …" "Don't do …" "Never …" "You must not …" and "You should …" are typically principles, as are statements given to guide human behavior, such as "Greet your customer courteously by name using a friendly greeting," "Listen with an open mind when your children tell you their problems," and other imperative statements.

Examples of Principles

- "The following five safety guidelines should always be followed when changing the main motor … [the principles are then stated]"
- "Never criticize the ideas of others during the brainstorming phase of the discussion."
- "Clients do not transact business with those they do not trust."
- "If workers have the knowledge, skills, tools, and opportunity to perform a task on the job but are still not performing, then look to motivational reasons for lack of performance, such as lack of incentives or the performance of the task leads to a punishing result (such as an increase in workload)."

- Ohm's law

Teaching *Behavioral* Principles

To teach *behavioral* principles, present the principle in the form of imperative statements or bulleted lists of rules or guidelines. Then provide examples as necessary to show how the rules are applied to real-life situations or applications. If appropriate and approved by management, provide motivational treatments to incent compliance with the guidelines, describing what students will gain or lose if they follow or fail to follow the rules.

Use the following additional guidelines in designing and teaching behavioral principles.

1. Present the principle as an imperative statement or a bulleted list of rules or guidelines.

State the principle in enough detail for the principle to be understood by your audience. If the statement of the principle contains terms, concepts, or other types of information that are unknown to your audience, then teach that information at this point in the instruction using strategies appropriate to its type.

2. Provide examples as needed to show how the rules are applied to real-life situations or applications.

Provide examples that show how the principle is applied in one or more instances. Examples help students see how the sometimes abstract directives that are given in a principle are interpreted and applied.

3. If appropriate and approved by management, provide motivational incentives.

If appropriate and if approved by management, set up incentives that encourage students to comply with the principle back in the workplace. Inform students of these incentives during training. This can help motivate students to learn the principle during training.

4. Provide students the opportunity to apply the principle and receive feedback.

As with other forms of learning, provide students the opportunity to practice the principle and apply it during training to build their confidence in their ability to follow the principle back on the job.

Example of Teaching a Behavioral Principle

When entering information on the Policy Payment screen, follow these guidelines:

- Enter data for all fields in red. These fields are required fields.
- After entering the policy number, verify that the name displayed is the same as the name on the payment coupon.
- Verify that the payment amount you entered is the same as the payment amount entered on the payment coupon by the customer.
- Do not press *Submit* before all required and desired optional fields are entered. Doing so creates a journal entry that must be manually corrected by the accounting department.

Failure to comply with these guidelines will trigger immediate management review of your performance whenever any of the following conditions hold:

- The wrong policy number was entered on three or more occasions.
- The wrong amount was entered on two or more occasions.
- Two or more manual journal corrections were required in any given month.

The following shows an example of a completed Policy Payment screen for customer John Doe, customer number 123456, who is making a payment of $765.45.

[An example is now presented]

Complete the following exercise …

Teaching *General* Principles

General principles are different from *behavioral* principles. General principles describe causal or logical relationships.

To teach general principles, follow these guidelines:

1. State the principle and define and describe each of the component elements.

If the general principle is a formula that shows the relationship between several items, define and describe each entry in the formula. For example, Ohm's law relates resistance, voltage, and amperes. Define each of these terms after stating the formula.

2. Provide an explanation for why the relationship holds or can be assumed to be true.

Explain why the logic holds or what evidence leads to the conclusion. For example, explain why sales and client rapport seem to be correlated. Providing explanations deepens students' understanding of the principle and will help them to remember the relationship.

3. Provide examples that illustrate the application of the principle.

Show several examples of the application of the principle. For example, if you are teaching electricians to wire a house, show how to apply Ohm's law to several residential wiring scenarios.

4. Provide students the opportunity to apply the principle and receive feedback.

Provide students the opportunity to practice (apply) the principle during training to build their confidence in their ability to follow it back on the job.

Example of teaching a general principle: Ohm's law

There are three important properties of electricity that are involved in circuit analysis, design, and testing: resistance, voltage, and amperes. Resistance is ... Voltage is ... Amperes is ... Scientists have discovered that these three properties of electricity are related by a mathematical equation called Ohm's law. Ohm's law states that resistance equals voltage divided by amperes:

$$R = V / A$$

Alternate and equivalent forms of Ohm's law are:

$$A = V / R \quad \text{and} \quad V = R * A$$

These alternative forms are mathematically equivalent statements, and one can be derived from the others.

Here are some examples of applying Ohm's law ...

Try your hand at applying Ohm's law in the following exercises.

Overview of Facts

Facts are simple assertions or statements that are assumed to be true. In contrast to concepts, facts stand on their own and do *not* represent classes of objects or ideas. Facts can be specifications, dates when events occurred, chronologies of events, proper names, names of places, symbols used to represent things, assertions about the truth or condition of something, "statements of fact," or specific data.

Examples of facts include:

- the temperature of the surface of the sun is ... ,
- press **F9** to start the spell check function,
- the Greek letter п is used to represent the irrational number pi,
- the ABC printer outputs 20 pages per minute of laser-quality output,
- the coldest temperatures recorded in the 48 contiguous states occurred on Mt. Washington in New England on ... ,
- the specifications for the model 800 are ... ,

- the sales order entry program is invoked from the desktop by clicking the **Sales Entry** icon,
- the last company stock split occurred on ... , and
- the computer's central processing complex is located on the third tier of rack A.

Teaching Facts

Because facts are simple assertions or statements, there are no complex rules for teaching them.

To teach facts, follow these guidelines:

1. Write clear, precise statements.

Make each statement accurate, clear, and complete.

2. As appropriate, provide the context for understanding the factual statements.

Some facts might not be understood properly unless they are presented in proper context. For example, water boils at different temperatures according to the air pressure in which it is boiled. Water boils at a lower temperature on the top of a high mountain than at sea level.

3. Organize groups of related facts.

Organize related groups of facts, such as specifications for a machine, into subgroups and label them appropriately to make it easy to reference and remember them by subgroup. Within each subgroup, use bulleted lists or tables to further organize and present detailed individual facts.

4. If students will be required to remember facts, provide support for memory.

If the objectives call for students to remember facts by rote memory, incorporate memory strategies into the lesson to enhance retention (see part 1, "Understanding How Humans Learn," in my companion book, *Instructional*

Design—Step by Step: Nine Easy Steps for Designing Lean, Effective, and Motivational Instruction. Bloomington, IN: iUniverse, 2013.)

Example of presenting a related group of facts:

The ABC computer router supports the following specifications of interest to our customers:

Supported Network Interface Cards (NICs)

- Token Ring
- 10/100 Ethernet

Data Handling Capacity

- 100 MBS (model 1030)
- 500 MBS (model 1050)

Internal Memory

- 100 GB – 2 TB (model 1030)
- 500 GB – 5 TB (model 1050)

Overview of Structures

Structures are objects—physical or logical—that can be divided into component parts. The most obvious examples of structures are *physical* objects and their corresponding components, such as a diagram of a bicycle along with its corresponding parts. A structure can also be a *logical* entity that can be broken into its component pieces, such as an organizational chart.

Structures typically involve things you can draw, diagram, represent, or photograph. Structures tell the student what something looks like and what its parts are. They can also include a description of the functions of those parts.

Examples of structures include

- an organization chart,
- an exploded view of the parts of a machine,
- the grammatical structure of a sentence,

- a computer application screen with its component elements, such as menu bars, toolbars, status line, and title bar,
- the different layers of labeled rock strata in a diagram of the Grand Canyon, and
- the syntax of computer operating system commands.

Teaching Structures

Like facts, teaching structures is not complicated.

To teach structures, follow these guidelines:

1. Present an appropriate visual depiction of the structure.

Structures are always represented visually, so present an appropriate visual depiction of the structure, such as a photograph, diagram, block diagram, or illustration along with its component parts. If certain relationships exist among its components, such as a wheel assembly of a bicycle, then depict the correct relationship among the component parts, such as using a center line to show the order and relationship of the exploded parts. Be sure to provide a title or caption for the overall diagram.

2. Identify and label each of the parts of interest.

Do this so that the accompanying text or discussion can refer to the visually depicted parts.

3. Use special graphical techniques as appropriate.

Use graphical techniques such as exploded views, callouts, or other techniques as appropriate. If the structure is complex or has numerous parts, create a separate parts table that is keyed to the graphic. For complex structures, consider a layered approach that uses visual or logical layers to provide a comprehensive breakdown of the structure.

4. Follow the principles of good visual design.

See chapter 11 of this book and part 1, "Understanding How Humans Learn," in my companion book, *Instructional Design—Step by Step: Nine Easy Steps for Designing Lean, Effective, and Motivational Instruction*, for more information on visual design.

5. Provide supporting text or narration.

Provide supporting textual or verbal explanation of the structure to the level of detail that is required by the objectives of that topic or lesson. Graphical depictions alone can be frustrating or confusing—a fact that is confirmed by many of those who try to follow the pictures-only instructions that come with many gadgets and devices.

A simple example of teaching a structure:

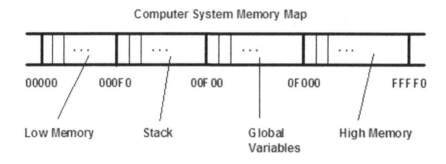

Figure 6. A simple example of a structure

Review of Classifications

Classifications are assignments of specific items into two or more categories using some kind of sorting criteria. Classifications usually include words such as *types of, kinds of, sorts of,* and *aspects of.*

Examples of classifications include

- kinds of financial loans;
- types of trees;

- types of network adapter cards;
- categories of user errors;
- kinds of age-related illnesses;
- types of postage for sending packages, letters, and parcels;
- types of sailboats; and
- categories of workers for human resource (HR) purposes, such as exempt, non-exempt, and so forth.

Teaching Classifications

To teach classifications, follow these guidelines:

1. Title the classification appropriately.

Use titles that start with "Types of," "Kinds of," "Sorts of," "Aspects of," and so forth so that students know immediately that they are dealing with a classification scheme.

2. Describe the class of objects to be classified.

This is usually included in the title, but it might need more explanation in the accompanying text. For example, if the title says "Types of trees," what is considered a tree and what is considered a bush or some other large plant?

3. State the possible classification categories.

Present the list or taxonomy of the various ways that the object can be classified. Presenting the list in its entirety, if possible, helps students see the inclusive list and compare the different categories.

4. Teach any enabling content that is necessary to apply the sorting criteria.

If the method for classifying objects into the various categories is beyond the entry-level skills and knowledge of the students, then teach the procedures for how to make the classification along with any enabling content, such as related concepts, principles, facts, and so forth. Make sure that the criteria for making the classification are clear and unambiguous.

5. If there is only one sorting criterion, then use a simple list to show the classification categories and criteria.

If only one simple criterion is used to classify objects into the various categories, use a simple list to show the classification. For example, bodily exercises can be classified into one of three types depending on the main purpose of the exercise:

Types of Exercises	
Exercise type	**Purpose of the exercise**
Aerobic	Work the cardiovascular system of the body
Strength	Build muscle mass
Stretching	Increase flexibility

6. If there are two or more sorting criteria, use a table or classification tree.

The best way to understand this principle is to see an example of it.

Example of teaching a more complex classification

Classifying Console Failures into Error Category Codes

Causes for failure of the XYZ system console can be classified into two main categories: network communication errors and hardware failures.

Network communication errors display a red flag in the communication status area of the status bar on the console.

Hardware failures do not show any indicators on the console, but display specific LED array readouts on the LED array unit inside of the back of the system. Use the color sequence of these three LEDs to determine the error category code according to the following table:

Types of Errors for the ABC System Console			
Error Type	**LED Array**	**Console Status Bar**	**Error Category Code**
Network Communication Error	—	Red flag in the COM status field of the main console	110
Hardware Failure	Green, Yellow, Green	—	512
	Green, Green, Yellow	—	525
	Yellow, Green, Green	—	527
	Red, Yellow, Red	—	530
	Yellow, Red, Red	—	531
	Red, Red, Red	—	535

Use the XYZ Service Manual to find the step-by-step problem determination procedures that correspond to each error category code.

Summary Insight: Creating Lean, Effective Instructional Presentations Is What Instructional Development Is All About

You have now learned how to classify information into one of seven types and how to design and create instructional presentations that optimize learning for each of those types. This is one of the most important and key skills of an instructional developer.

This skill involves asking yourself the following questions for each chunk of information that you must teach:

- What type of information is it?
- What is the research-based recommended strategy for teaching this type of information?

After classifying the information, you must then design and create a presentation that implements the instructional strategies for that type of information. These strategies will make it much easier for students to learn and remember the material.

The following book has entire chapters devoted to teaching procedures, concepts, facts, processes, and providing for transfer of learning to the workplace.

Developing Technical Training: A Structured Approach for Developing Classroom and Computer-Based Instructional Materials, 2nd Edition, Ruth C. Clark, Ed.D. Washington, D.C.: International Society for Performance Improvement, 1999, ISBN 1-890289-07-8.

This book is available from the online bookstore of the International Society for Performance Improvement at http://www.ispi.org.

Chapter Summary—Teaching Principles, Facts, Structures, and Classifications

This chapter discussed how to teach principles, facts, structures, and classifications—four of the seven types of information.

You should now be able to

- define and describe the two types of principles and give several examples of them,
- list the major instructional elements that you should include in teaching principles,
- do the following in teaching behavioral principles:
  - explain how to present the principle and why it is important to provide examples of its application,
  - explain when motivational incentives should be provided in the workplace to motivate learning of the principles during training,
  - describe why it is important to provide students the opportunity to apply the principle and receive feedback,
- do the following in teaching general principles:
  - explain how to state the principle and define and describe each of the component elements,
  - explain why it is important to provide an explanation for why the relationship holds or can be assumed to be true and to provide examples that illustrate the application of the principle,
  - explain why it is important to provide students the opportunity to apply the principle and receive feedback,
- define and describe facts and give several examples of them,
- do the following in teaching facts:
  - describe why it is important to write clear, precise statements,
  - describe why you should provide the context of the facts,
  - describe how to organize groups of related facts,
  - explain why you should provide memory support if students are required to remember the facts,
- define and describe the two types of structures and give several examples of each,

- do the following in teaching structures:
  - describe how to present an appropriate visual depiction of the structure,
  - explain why it is important to identify and label each of the parts of interest,
  - describe how to use special graphical techniques as appropriate,
  - explain why it is important to follow the principles of good visual design,
  - explain why you should provide supporting text or narration,
- define and describe classifications and give several examples of classifications,
- list the types of words or phrases that are typically used in classification titles,
- do the following in teaching classifications:
  - describe how to properly title the classification,
  - explain how to describe the class of objects to be classified,
  - describe why you should list the possible classification categories,
  - describe why you must teach any enabling content that is necessary to apply the sorting criteria, and
- state the two questions that instructional developers should ask about each chunk of information that they have to teach in a lesson or topic.

Check Your Understanding

1. **True or false? General principles tell a person what should or should not be done in various circumstances; behavioral principles describe causal or logical relationships, such as what can be concluded in light of the evidence.**

2. **True or false? In teaching principles, you should provide examples that show how the principle can be applied to one or more applications.**

3. **True or false? Management-approved incentives can be used to encourage students to learn behavioral principles during training and apply them in the workplace.**

4. **In teaching general principles, you should: (Select all that apply.)**

    A. Provide students the opportunity to apply the principle and receive feedback.

    B. Present the principle as an imperative statement or a bulleted list of rules or guidelines.

    C. Provide examples that illustrate the application of the principle.

    D. Provide an explanation for why the relationship holds or can be assumed to be true.

    E. Provide motivational incentives, if appropriate and approved by management.

    F. State the principle and define and describe each of the principle's component elements.

5. **True or false? Facts are simple assertions or statements that are assumed to be true; they stand on their own and do not represent classes of objects or ideas as do concepts.**

6. **In teaching facts, you should: (Select all that apply.)**

    A. Provide students the opportunity to apply the fact and receive feedback.

    B. Organize groups of related facts.

    C. Provide examples of the facts.

    D. Provide support for memory if students will be required to remember facts.

    E. Write clear, precise statements.

    F. Present the fact as an imperative statement or a bulleted list of rules or guidelines.

    G. Provide the context for the fact.

7. **The two types of structures are _____ structures and _____ structures.**

8. **True or false? Structures typically involve things you can draw, diagram, represent, or photograph.**

9. **In teaching structures, you should: (Select all that apply.)**

    A. Use special graphical techniques as appropriate.

    B. Follow the principles of good visual design.

C. Present the structure as an imperative statement or a bulleted list of rules or guidelines.

D. Present an appropriate visual depiction of the structure.

E. Provide supporting text or narration.

F. Identify and label each of the parts of interest.

10. **Titles that include phrases such as "types of," "kinds of," "sorts of," and "aspects of" indicate a _____ type of information.**

11. **In teaching classifications, you should: (Select all that apply.)**

A. Teach any enabling content that is necessary to apply the sorting criteria.

B. Describe the class of objects to be classified.

C. If there are two or more sorting criteria, use a table or classification tree.

D. If there is only one sorting criterion, then use a simple list.

E. State the possible classification categories.

F. Title the classification appropriately.

12. **In creating an instructional presentation for a chunk of enabling content, you should ask yourself which two questions? (Select two.)**

A. What do I think is the best way to teach this information?

B. Is this information that the subject matter experts wanted in the training?

C. What type of information is it?

D. Why is this information being included?

E. Where did the information come from?

F. What is the research-based recommended strategy for teaching this type of information?

Answers

1. False. *Behavioral* principles tell a person what should or should not be done in various circumstances; *general* principles describe causal or logical relationships, such as what can be concluded in light of the evidence.
2. True
3. True
4. A, C, D, and F
5. True
6. B, D, E, and G
7. The correct answer is "physical" and "logical."
8. True
9. A, B, D, E, and F
10. The correct answer is "classification."
11. A, B, C, D, E, and F
12. C and F

CHAPTER 7:

Creating the Remaining Instructional Events and Finalizing the Topic

This chapter discusses the next step in the instructional development process—how to create the instructional events that were dictated by the instructional design document and finalize the topic.

Where We Are At in the Instructional Development Process

This chapter discusses step 3 and in the development process—how to create the instructional events that were dictated by the instructional design document and finalize the topic.

1. Perform an analysis of the objectives to determine all enabling content.

2. Classify information into its type and create corresponding instructional presentations.

3. **Create the remaining instructional events and finalize the topic.**

4. Create scripts (for technology-based training).

5. Perform a quality check on the training materials.

6. Pilot and revise all course materials.

Review of Instructional Events

Instructional events are learning strategies and activities that are built into the training that are specifically designed to facilitate and promote learning.

Examples of instructional events and activities

Presenting information is itself an instructional event, if it has been designed according to sound instructional design principles. **Note:** For information on *designing* instructional presentations, see my companion book to this book, *Instructional Design – Step by Step: Nine Easy Steps for Designing Lean, Effective, and Motivational Instruction*. Bloomington, IN: iUniverse, 2013.

In addition to the main presentation materials, other instructional events include

- reading or listening to introductions and summaries,
- answering questions,
- performing individual exercises,
- watching demonstrations,
- solving problems,
- taking quizzes and exams,
- participating in group discussions and exercises,
- interacting within a case study on a computer,
- using tools or new equipment,
- role playing with fellow students,
- watching a video,
- viewing an animation or Flash sequence,
- playing an instructional game,
- observing expert performers,

- going through an online simulation,
- teaching others,
- completing a mentorship,
- making presentations,
- writing a paper,
- performing real work (usually, in a protected, "safe" environment), and
- interacting with a virtual world

Review of Specifications for Instructional Events

The designs for instructional events that are found in the instructional design document are blueprints or skeletons of the events. They should specify enough detail about the event that an instructional developer can write or create the event after gathering the source material. Indeed, the instructional design document should

- identify *where* instructional events are needed in the course,
- determine *what* each event will be (its type, such as an exercise or quiz), and
- *design* (write the specifications for) the instructional event.

Specifications for an instructional event or activity typically include

- the name of the activity;
- an overall summary or high-level description of the activity;
- the purpose of the activity;
- the structure of the activity (specific events and their sequence and format, such as "a numbered series of steps for students to follow");
- a detailed outline or description of the content of the activity, such as the specific functions or tasks to be exercised;
- any templates that should be followed when developing the activity;
- for events that employ questions, specifications for those questions, such as the number of questions, types of allowable questions, how many questions per instructional segment or topic, and how the questions will be administered, scored, and reported;

- for instructor-led training, the design for this piece of the instructor exercise guide, if one is needed, that gives specific directions to the instructor on how to conduct the activity (for example, details on how to set up student group sessions, group presentations, and wrap-up class discussions); and
- references to where the source material for the activity can be found.

To learn more about *designing* instructional events, see chapter 14, "Designing Practice Exercises and Other Instructional Events," in my companion book, *Instructional Design—Step by Step: Nine Easy Steps for Designing Lean, Effective, and Motivational Instruction.* Bloomington, IN: iUniverse, 2013.

Creating the Remaining Instructional Events and Finalizing the Topic

In this step of the instructional development process, you perform the following tasks:

- **Write, script, or create the instructional events using the specifications contained in the instructional design document.**

  The specifications in the instructional design document do not contain all of the detailed content or source material that you will need to develop the event. Find or solicit source material from subject matter experts or perform research to learn the material yourself so that you can write or script the actual instructional event.

- **Decide whether to refresh additional prerequisite information.**

  The instructional analysis is completed during development. This analysis might uncover detailed prerequisite information that needs to be refreshed. If so, provide an instructional event to refresh that information. **Note:**

Prerequisite information is any information that the student must know to understand the material that is about to be presented.

- **Determine the final order or sequence of events.**

  Decide the order in which to present all of the instructional presentations and events in the lesson.

Note: The principles of grammar, style, usage, good writing, and the techniques for writing or scripting specific instructional events, such as group activities, role plays, multimedia presentations, videos, Flash animations, test questions, and so forth, are not covered in this book. Please consult other sources for additional information on these topics.

Deciding Whether to Refresh Additional Prerequisite Information

As you continue the instructional and content analyses that were begun during instructional design, you might identify a need to refresh additional prerequisite information that was not already listed to be refreshed by the instructional design document. This prerequisite information might have already been taught in a previous lesson in the course, or it might be part of the assumed entry-level knowledge and skills of your audience. During development, you must decide if it needs to be refreshed before you present the main lesson content.

In deciding what information to refresh, you should ask yourself, "How likely are students to remember the information at the level of detail that is required in this lesson?" If they are not likely to remember, then consider providing an activity that refreshes the information.

Factors to Consider in Determining If Information Should Be Refreshed

As discussed in the Part 1, "Understanding How Humans Learn," in my companion book, *Instructional Design—Step by Step: Nine Easy Steps for Designing Lean, Effective, and Motivational Instruction*, information is subject to extinction—

the inability to recall the information—as time passes. Therefore, you cannot assume that students will remember every concept, procedure, or other piece of information that was previously taught.

Consider refreshing prerequisite information when one or more of the following factors are present:

- significant time has passed since students first learned the information,
- the information is complex and detailed,
- students were given little or no practice using the information,
- students were not asked to recall the information,
- the information was not stored away in memory very strongly (few learning events or memory strategies were provided to strengthen and reinforce memory and the recall of the information),
- a significant amount of other information has been taught since students' initial exposure to the information, or
- the information is critical or key.

Determining the Final Sequence of Instructional Events in the Topic

After you have created your instructional materials for a lesson, you must then finalize their sequence within the lesson. This is necessary because the instructional design document only provides the sequence for higher-level concepts and instructional events for a lesson or module. During instructional development, you perform additional instructional and content analyses that reveals the remaining enabling content for the lesson. This content must then be sequenced.

After you perform your analysis, if you believe that you need to change the sequence of events that was specified in the instructional design document, discuss your proposed changes with the instructional designer.

The Three Rules of Sequencing

Follow these guidelines to determine the sequence of instructional events within a lesson:

1. Teach prerequisite knowledge before it is first needed.

This is the first rule of sequencing. Prerequisite information is any information that the student must know to understand the material that is about to be presented. Students become quickly frustrated and their learning is impaired when prerequisite information is not taught first. For example, teach the definition of the irrational number *pi* before teaching the formula for the area of a circle that uses it.

2. Teach prerequisite information just before it is needed, except in special circumstances.

As a general rule, teach prerequisite information just before the point at which it is needed. This will ensure that the information is fresh in students' short-term memories when it is needed. However, sometimes there are special circumstances that dictate that prerequisite information be taught earlier in the lesson along with other prerequisite information. For example, rather than teaching the different aspects of computer networks in scattered locations throughout a lesson or unit, it might be better to teach the overall concept of a computer network as an integrated whole upfront in the lesson or unit.

3. Follow Gagne's events of instruction in sequencing lessons or topics.

As presented in chapter 5, "Ten Key Teaching Principles" in my companion book, *Instructional Design—Step by Step: Nine Easy Steps for Designing Lean, Effective, and Motivational Instruction*, Gagne's eight events of instruction are:

1. **Gain attention:** Get students to focus on the instruction being presented.

2. **Stimulate recall of prerequisite information:** Review prerequisite information that students must understand before they will be able to understand what you are about to present.
3. **Present the stimulus:** Present the new information or material to be learned.
4. **Guide thinking:** Provide cognitive strategies, organizers, emphasis techniques, and so forth to facilitate cognitive processing, learning, and retention.
5. **Elicit performance:** Have students practice the skill and knowledge you are teaching.
6. **Provide feedback:** Provide individual feedback on each student's performance.
7. **Provide generalizing experiences:** Help students generalize, transfer, and apply concepts, procedures, and practices to the real world or to a broader application.
8. **Assess performance:** Provide an assessment to measure how well the student can perform the task or the objectives.

A Template for Sequencing a Topic

The following sequence of events is a typical flow for a topic or lesson:

- introduction and overview
  - gain attention and discuss the relevance, importance, objectives, transition, context, and any organizing structures or frameworks.
- instructional segment 1
  - provide transition, context, and information on why the material is relevant
  - refresh prerequisite information
  - present new information, graphics, events, or multimedia with guidance
  - demonstrate skills or give examples of concepts and principles
  - provide practice with feedback
  - provide a self-assessment (quiz, performance assessment, or checkpoint questions, as appropriate)

- instructional segments 2, 3, . . . N
- integrative exercise
- lesson summary or review
- lesson assessment (if required by the client)

Example of how a lesson was sequenced

<u>Lesson Objective</u>

- Given previously unseen information of various types, correctly classify the information into its type.

<u>Lesson Sequence</u>

- introduction and overview
- presentation: What are information types?
- presentation: Definitions and examples of the seven information types
- game: Associating definitions with their information type
- presentation: How to classify information into its type
- instructor demonstration: Classifying information into its type
- exercise: Classifying information into its type
- quiz: Classifying information into its type
- discussion, summary, and final wrap up

Additional Factors That Can Influence Sequencing

Other factors that can influence how you organize and sequence information include

- **the type of information** that is being taught (for example, procedures are sequenced by their numbered steps; processes are sequenced by their stages or flow over time),
- **the relationship between the information** (set/subset, part/whole, cause/effect, or organizational—many of these relationships were identified in your instructional and content analyses),
- **the priority** of the information (high to low or low to high),

- **the physical structure or layout of the information** (for example, the location of individual car parts in a car), and
- **the functional purposes or groupings that exist in the information** (for example, in computer application training, groups of related functions for editing information, viewing information, and inserting new information).

Chapter Summary—Creating the Instructional Events and Finalizing the Topic

This chapter discussed the next step in the instructional development process—how to create the instructional events that were dictated by the instructional design document and finalize the topic.

You should now be able to

- define instructional events and provide several examples of them,
- describe the level of detail that is found in the instructional design document for instructional events,
- list and describe the three tasks that are performed in step 3 of the instructional development process: Create the remaining instructional events and finalize the topic,
- describe why you must decide if additional prerequisite information needs to be refreshed,
- list several factors to consider in determining if information should be refreshed,
- describe why the instructional developer determines the final sequence of instructional events in a lesson or topic,
- state and explain the three rules of sequencing,
- describe how Gagne's events of instruction support a simple model of learning,
- present and explain a typical sequence of events in a topic or lesson, and
- list and explain additional factors that can influence sequencing.

Check Your Understanding (1 of 3)

1. **True or false? Instructional events are the insights or "ah ha" moments that students have while taking the training in which they finally understand the information.**

2. **True or false? The design specifications for instructional events that are documented in the instructional design document should**

specify enough detail about the event that an instructional developer can write or create the event after gathering the source material.

3. **As part of the step 3 in the instructional development process—create the remaining instructional events—you must: (Select all that apply.)**

    A. Write or create the instructional events using the specifications contained in the instructional design document.

    B. Perform a quality check on the materials that you have created.

    C. Pilot the training and make revisions based on the feedback received.

    D. Decide whether to refresh additional prerequisite information.

    E. Complete the instructional and content analyses that was started during instructional design.

    F. Determine the final order or sequence of events.

4. **True or false? All of the prerequisite information that needs to be refreshed is identified in the instructional design document.**

5. **True or false? It is possible that the prerequisite information for a lesson might not have been taught in a previous lesson.**

6. **Which of the following factors should be considered in determining whether prerequisite information should be refreshed? (Select all that apply.)**

    A. Students were given little or no practice using the information.

    B. The information is critical or key.

    C. The development effort that was required to first teach the information was large.

    D. Significant time has passed since students first learned the information.

    E. The number of checkpoint questions that you are planning to include in the topic.

    F. A significant amount of other information has been taught since students' initial exposure to the information.

7. **True or false? All sequencing of instructional presentations, events, and information is defined in the instructional design document.**

8. **The three rules of sequencing a lesson or topic are: (Select all that apply.)**
    A. Prerequisite information is best taught at the beginning of the topic or lesson.
    B. Teach prerequisite information just before it is needed, except in special circumstances.
    C. Follow the sequence of Gagne's events of instruction.
    D. Follow the sequence given in Horn's information types.
    E. Teach prerequisite knowledge before it is first needed.
    F. Follow your own instincts.

9. **True or false? The sequence of instructional events prescribed by Gagne is:**
    1. Gain attention
    2. Stimulate recall of prerequisite information
    3. Present the stimulus
    4. Elicit performance
    5. Guide thinking
    6. Assess performance
    7. Provide feedback
    8. Provide generalizing experiences

10. **What is wrong with the following lesson template? (Select all that apply.)**
    - Instructional segment 1
        - Provide transition, context, and information on why the material is relevant
        - Refresh prerequisite information
        - Present new information, graphics, events, or multimedia with guidance
        - Demonstrate skills or give examples of concepts and principles
        - Provide practice with feedback

- Provide a self-assessment (quiz, performance assessment, or checkpoint questions, as appropriate)
- Instructional segments 2, 3, . . . N
- Integrative exercise

A. The instructional events within "Instructional segment 1" are out of order.

B. It has no topic summary.

C. It has no topic assessment (if the client requires an assessment).

D. It should include only one instructional segment per lesson or topic.

E. It has no topic introduction and overview.

F. It is too general to be of any use.

11. **True or false? The type of information that you are teaching can influence how you sequence the information within a lesson or topic.**

Answers

1. False. Instructional events are learning strategies and activities that are built into the training that are specifically designed to facilitate and promote learning.

2. True

3. A, D, and F

4. False. When you continue the instructional and content analyses that were begun during instructional design, you might realize the need to refresh additional prerequisite information that was not already tagged by the instructional design document to be refreshed.

5. True. It might be part of the assumed entry-level knowledge and skills of your audience, or you might have neglected to teach the information in your course.

6. A, B, D, and F

7. False. The instructional design document only provides the sequence for higher-level concepts and instructional events in a lesson or topic. During instructional development, you perform additional instructional

and content analyses to reveal the remaining enabling content for the topic. This content must then be sequenced.

8. B, C, and E

9. This statement is false. The correct order is:
   1. Gain attention
   2. Stimulate recall of prerequisite information
   3. Present the stimulus
   4. Guide thinking
   5. Elicit performance
   6. Provide feedback
   7. Provide generalizing experiences
   8. Assess performance

10. B, C, and E

11. True. For example, procedures are sequenced by their numbered steps; processes are sequenced by their stages and flow over time.

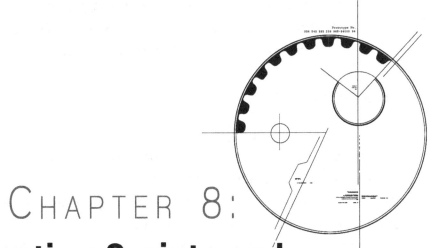

CHAPTER 8:
Creating Scripts and Performing a Quality Check

This chapter discusses the next two steps in the instructional development process: how to create scripts and how to perform a quality check on your instructional materials.

Where We Are At in the Instructional Development Process

This chapter discusses steps 4 and 5 in the development process—how to write scripts and how to perform a quality check on the training materials.

1. Perform an analysis of the objectives to determine all enabling content.
2. Classify information into its type and create corresponding instructional presentations.
3. Create the remaining instructional events and finalize the topic.

4. Create scripts (for technology-based training).

5. Perform a quality check on the training materials.

6. Pilot and revise all course materials.

Creating Scripts

Step 4 in the development process applies only to technology-based training, such as web-based training, video, or multimedia presentations. For technology-based training, the instructional developer creates a script for each topic, lesson, or event. Scripts provide technology professionals, graphic artists, and others with all of the information—content and interaction descriptions—that they need to build the presentations and interactions. For example, a script for web-based training specifies things such as

- the screen or event number,
- the title to be displayed on the screen,
- the type of screen (templates are usually created for each screen type),
- specifications for any graphics to be displayed on the screen,
- the text to be displayed on the screen,
- descriptions of any special interactions that the student can or must take on the screen,
- graphic file names,
- alt-text descriptions for graphical accessibility compliance, and
- the instructional prompts that tell the student what to do on that particular screen.

When Are Scripts Created During the Instructional Development Process?

For non-technology-based training, steps 2 and 3 of the instructional development process—classify information into its type, create corresponding instructional presentations, and create the remaining instructional events—is where the training materials are actually created.

For technology-based training, the instructional developer does not usually create the final training deliverables during steps 2 and 3. Instead, the developer creates a script using a word processor or an authoring tool for the delivery technology. The script is then given to others who are specialists in that technology. These specialists then create the final training deliverables using authoring tools, applications, and languages.

For example, the instructional developer writes a script for a web-based training course. This script is then given to a courseware engineer who is an expert in authoring web-based training presentations using a particular authoring tool. The courseware engineer then creates the final web-based training program.

Using Script Templates

Instructional developers often use templates to help them create scripts for technology-based training. Script templates are forms or shell documents. They follow a set format that provides places for the developer to describe the major elements for each type of screen or interaction that might be used in a course. The developer copies this template and uses it to create the script for a specific lesson or topic or the script for an instructional event, such an interactive Flash animation.

For example, one page in the script template might contain a boilerplate screen for a true/false checkpoint question. When developers want to include a true/false checkpoint question in their scripts, they copy this page and insert it into their script at the appropriate location. This simplifies the creation of the script and helps ensure consistency across the course for screens of the same type.

Scripts for time-based, highly interactive, or media intensive events, such as Flash animations or video, have their own special scripting requirements. For scripting requirements and templates in those technologies, consult qualified professionals in those technologies.

A Partial Example of a Script for a Topic in a Web-based Training Course

To see a partial example of a script for a topic in a web-based training course, please see appendix A.

Performing a Quality Check on Your Instructional Materials

In step 4 of the development process, you perform a quality check on all of the training materials that you have developed. This step can be broken into two sets of tasks: Tasks that you perform, and tasks that others perform.

Tasks that you perform:

- validate your materials against the instructional design, and
- review your materials using a training development checklist.

Reviews that you will solicit the help of others to perform:

- subject matter expert (SME) review,
- instructional designer review,
- editor review,
- accessibility expert review, and
- functional tester review (if training is technology-based).

Validating Your Materials against the Instructional Design

The purpose of validation is to make sure that the training course was indeed created in accordance with the design specified in the instructional design document.

To validate your training materials against the instructional design:

1. **Review all of the objectives and ask yourself, "Were all of the objectives addressed?"**

   Systematically go through the list of detailed objectives for each lesson or topic one by one and verify that each objective has been taught in the instructional events and materials. In this step, you are looking for missing teaching materials for objectives that were overlooked during development.

2. **Review all of the training materials and ask yourself, "Do all of the training materials directly support one or more of the lesson objectives?"**

In this step, you do the converse of step 1. Systematically go through each part of the lesson and see if that part directly supports (is *required* enabling content for) the teaching of one of the lesson's objectives. In this step, you are not looking for *missing* materials as in the previous task, but for *extraneous* materials—presentations, activities, and events that are *not* needed because they do not directly support the accomplishment of *any* of the objectives of the lesson.

Why you must perform *both* steps 1 and 2:

The questions that are asked in these two steps are independent of one another. It is possible to have missing content, extraneous content, or both.

Consider the following examples:

Example: All of the materials support the lesson objectives, but there are objectives for which there is no lesson material (missing content).

Example: All of the objectives are covered, but there is material that does not directly support the attainment of any of the objectives (extraneous content).

Example: There are objectives for which there is no lesson material (missing content), *and* there is material that does not directly support the attainment of any of the objectives (extraneous content).

3. **Do the lessons, units, and course "flesh out" or embody the design that is specified in the instructional design document?**

Check to see if you have followed the course structure and design as specified in the instructional design document. Was the intent and purpose of the instructional events carried out? Did you provide exercises where they were specified and create them as designed? Are you confident that students will be able to perform the objectives after they have completed the training?

4. **For each objective, ask yourself, "Are all of the instructional events that are required to master this objective present in the materials?"**

   In addition to the main instructional presentations, are all of the instructional *events*—such as exercises, quizzes, demonstrations, simulations, and so forth—that are required to master this objective present in the materials?

Reviewing Your Materials Using a Development Checklist

Training professionals and organizations often develop their own quality checklists that developers must use to assess the quality of their training materials. Entries that might be found on these checklists include:

1. **Did you talk to your audience?**

   Do your homework to see things from your audience's perspective. Then, write from that perspective. Avoid institutional or stuffy writing styles. Use examples, analogies, words, and sentences that your audience can relate to. Write as if a person from the audience were directly in front of you. Talk to them, speak their language, and mentor them.

2. **Did you write simply and concisely—for clarity and understanding—not to impress?**

   Avoid overly technical or academic-style discourse.

An excellent reference on writing simply and concisely is the classic book, *The Elements of Style, 4th edition*, by William Strunk Jr. and E. B. White, New York: Longman, 2000, ISBN 0-205-30902-X.

3. **Did you provide a smooth and logical flow?**

   Provide a smooth and logical flow at all levels in the course—at the course, unit, lesson, section, paragraph, and sentence levels. Teach prerequisite information immediately before the information that depends on it. Provide explicit transitions where content, context, or logic flow changes occur. During development, flip back and forth between prior slides, screens, or materials to ensure that you have provided a smooth and logical flow from the previous material to the current material.

4. **Were you consistent?**

   Use parallel grammatical structures in lists and headers. Create similar titles for similar information. Create titles and headers that are consistent with the overall framework or conceptual model given earlier in the course. Define and maintain a consistent visual layout and design.

5. **Did you emphasize key information?**

   Place key information in the foreground (larger, bolder, center, top of hierarchy, and so forth). Layer details or make them subordinate to key information. Teach only essential information—reference the rest. Tell students why the information is key information. Reinforce key ideas with graphics or instructional interactions. Review, refresh, and practice key information repeatedly over time.

6. **Did you support the cognitive learning process in all your materials?**

Follow all of the principles of learning, teaching, and instructional design given in my companion book, *Instructional Design—Step by Step: Nine Easy Steps for Designing Lean, Effective, and Motivational Instruction*.

7. **Did you try out any instructions in your training as if you were a student?**

   Try out step-by-step instructions before your students do! Sometimes developers never perform the instructions or procedures that provide to see if those instructions are correct and if any critical information is missing.

8. **Did you set your first draft aside for a period of time and then review it again later?**

   Take a fresh look at what you have written a day or two after you first created it. When you are mentally fresh, you will often see improvements that you could not previously see. The creative act of mentally composing information is often best accomplished when uninterrupted, at least initially. Return later to clean up, tighten, and improve what you have written.

9. **Did you assume a higher-level of entry knowledge and skill than what students actually have when they take the training?**

   Check that your materials do not assume that students possess skills or knowledge—such as acronyms, terms, concepts, procedures, facts, or ideas—that they do not know when they enter the training.

10. **Did you take personal responsibility for outstanding development?**

    Be a true professional and do a good job creating your training materials the first time around. Do not be lazy, careless, or sloppy in developing your content and then expect others, such as editors, SMEs, instructional designers, and reviewers, to fix your materials and make them well-written, well-presented, and instructionally sound.

Having Your Instructional Materials Reviewed by Others

As part of performing a quality check on your training materials, you should have your instructional materials reviewed by other professionals.

1. **Submit your materials to your subject matter experts (SMEs) for a technical accuracy review.**

   Ask your SMEs to review your training materials for technical accuracy. Tell them specifically what the purpose of their review is and make it clear that they are *not* reviewing the course to see if they personally like the way the training was designed, to suggest additional favorite content, or to redesign the course. Lay out expectations, set deadlines, establish mark-up procedures, and explain tracking and reporting procedures.

2. **Submit your materials to the instructional designer for a final review.**

   The instructional designer should review your training materials to make sure that the instructional design was properly implemented and that the detailed presentations and instructional events are instructionally sound.

3. **Submit your materials for editing.**

   Editors perform many services. For example, they check for misspellings, typos, grammatical problems, style issues, usage issues, inconsistencies in design and layout, and potential copyright infringements. Having another pair of eyes read the materials can also help uncover early problems students might have in understanding the instruction.

4. **Submit your materials for an accessibility test and review.**

   To assure that your materials comply with the needs of the disabled and with current accessibility laws, submit your materials to a team of professional accessibility testers and reviewers who can test your course for accessibility using screen readers, web checkers, and other tools. Fix any accessibility issues that they uncover.

5. **Submit your materials for a functional test.**

   For technology-based training, submit your materials to a team of testers who will perform comprehensive or representative use case testing on your course to ensure that functions, navigational methods, links, and interactions work as designed.

6. **Accept feedback without being defensive.**

   Be eager and willing to receive constructive feedback on your work from others without becoming defensive. Being defensive makes it less likely that others will agree to review or critique your work in the future. Recognize that the feedback you receive will not only improve your current training deliverables, but will improve and hone your professional skills.

Chapter Summary—Creating Scripts and Performing a Quality Check

This chapter discussed the next two steps in the instructional development process: how to create scripts and how to perform a quality check on your instructional materials.

You should now be able to

- define training scripts and list the types of entries that are typically found in a script for web-based training;
- describe when scripts are created in the instructional development process;
- define script templates and describe how instructional developers use them;
- list the tasks that are involved in performing a quality check on your instructional materials;
- list and describe the five steps for validating your instructional materials against the instructional design;
- describe why it is possible to have both missing content and extraneous content in the same topic or lesson;

- define development checklists, describe how developers use them, and provide several examples of entries that might appear in them;
- list and describe the five types of reviews that are performed by professionals other than yourself (the instructional developer); and
- describe why it is important to accept feedback without being defensive.

Check Your Understanding

1. **True or false? Scripts provide technology experts and other professionals with all of the information they need to build the presentation or event.**

2. **True or false? Scripts are created in the development process immediately before the enabling information is classified into its type.**

3. **True or false? Script templates contain the major script elements for each type of screen or interaction that the developer might choose to use in a lesson or topic.**

4. **Indicate which of the following tasks are performed by the developer and which are performed by others.**
   A. Perform an accessibility review
   B. Validate the materials against the instructional design
   C. Perform an editorial review
   D. Perform a functional test review
   E. Review the materials using a development checklist
   F. Perform a technical accuracy review
   G. Perform a final instructional design review

5. **True or false? The purpose of validation in the quality review stage of instructional development is to ensure that the training course was created in conformance with the instructional design.**

6. **True or false? It is impossible for a topic to have both missing content and extraneous content.**

7. **To talk directly to the student in your training materials, you should: (Select all that apply.)**

A. Write as if you are talking directly to students.

B. Do your homework to see things from your audience's perspective; then, write from that perspective.

C. Use passive voice in your writing as much as possible.

D. Avoid institutional or stuffy writing styles.

E. Use examples, analogies, words, and sentences that your audience can relate to.

F. Write as if a person from the audience were directly in front of you.

8. **You should provide explicit transitions in your materials where there are transitions in: (Select all that apply.)**

A. The flow of logic

B. Voice (active to passive or passive to active)

C. Context

D. Content

E. Tone of writing

9. **True or false? Setting aside the first draft of your materials and reviewing them again when you are mentally fresh can help you see improvements that you could not previously see.**

10. **True or false? In developing training, it is more efficient to quickly throw the materials together and rely on others—such as editors, SMEs, instructional designers, and reviewers—to improve upon them than it is to do a quality job of creating the materials in the first place.**

11. **As an instructional developer, after you have developed your training materials, you should submit them for review to: (Select all that apply.)**

A. At least two other instructional developers

B. The instructional designer for the course

C. An editor

D. Your subject matter experts (SMEs)

E. Accessibility testers

F. Functional testers (for technology-based training)

12. **True or false? Accessibility testing is performed to ensure that students in the target audience can enroll in and access the course over the web using their personal computers.**

Answers

1. True
2. False. Scripts are created after you have classified enabling content into its type and are designing and developing the instructional presentations or events. You then give your scripts to other professionals who do the actual building of the training materials.
3. True
4. A, tasks that others perform; B, tasks that the developer performs; C, tasks that others perform; D, tasks that others perform; E, tasks that the developer performs; F, tasks that others perform; and G, tasks that others perform.
5. True
6. False. It *is* possible for a topic to have both missing content and extraneous content.
7. A, B, D, E, and F
8. A, C, and D
9. True
10. False
11. B, C, D, E, and F
12. False. Accessibility testing is done to assure that your materials meet the needs of the disabled (such as those with visual or hearing impairments) and with current accessibility laws.

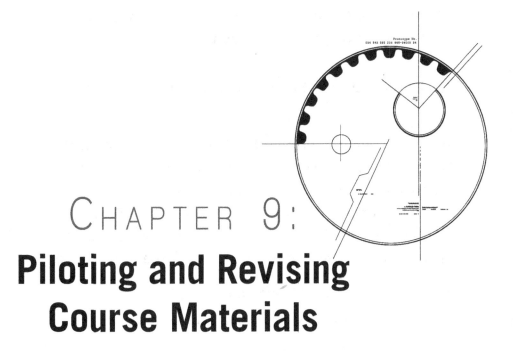

CHAPTER 9:
Piloting and Revising
Course Materials

This chapter presents the final step in the instructional development process: how to conduct a pilot and revise the course based on the feedback gathered during the pilot.

Where We Are At in the Instructional Development Process

This chapter discusses step 6 in the development process—how to pilot and revise the course materials.

1. Perform an analysis of the objectives to determine all enabling content.
2. Classify information into its type and create corresponding instructional presentations.
3. Create the remaining instructional events and finalize the topic.
4. Create scripts (for technology-based training).

5. Perform a quality check on the training materials.

6. Pilot and revise all course materials.

What Is a Course Pilot and Why Is It Important?

A course pilot is an early tryout of the course with *representative students* from the training audience. By "representative students," we mean students from each of the audience subgroups that were identified during requirements gathering (for more information on requirements gathering, see my companion book, *Instructional Design—Step by Step: Nine Easy Steps for Designing Lean, Effective, and Motivational Instruction*). During and after the pilot, student performance is assessed and student feedback is solicited.

Piloting the training can help you:

- Assess whether the training is effective and accomplished its objectives. For example:
  - Can students demonstrate that they can perform the target objectives after completing the course?
  - Can they transfer their newly acquired skills back to the job and apply them in the real world to produce the desired job outcomes and work products or accomplishments?
  - **Note:** These questions are very important not only to the designers and developers of the training, but to the sponsors of the training.
- Improve the training materials.

Direct observations of students can also be made that can uncover problem areas, misunderstandings, incomplete information, and so forth.

Conducting a Course Pilot

To pilot your training, follow these guidelines:

1. **Select students representatively from the target audience who have taken the required prerequisites and who possess the assumed entry-level skills and knowledge.**

Training is customized to a particular audience and to a specific set of needs. Therefore, it is critical that you pilot your course on students from *each* of your major target audience groupings. For example, pilot a sales course using sales students, not IT students. Using students from the wrong audience invalidates the results of the pilot and can frustrate the students who participate in the pilot. Choose students for pilot testing who have taken the prerequisite training that is required for the course and who possess the assumed entry level skills and knowledge.

2. **Create a climate conducive to giving feedback.**

   Brief students before they take the training. Explain that it is the training materials that are being tested, not the students. Explain that you will welcome any feedback that they can provide, discuss the value of that feedback, and tell students how it will be used to improve the training. When students do make comments, express your appreciation for those comments. Avoid any hint of defensiveness.

3. **Solicit feedback regularly.**

   Do not wait until the end of the course to solicit feedback. Students will have trouble remembering a particular paragraph or graphic that was unclear that they encountered several hours or days before. As a general guideline, solicit feedback at least after every lesson and more often as need dictates. If possible, watch students as they take the training and ask questions when they appear confused or frustrated. Keep a log of the questions that students ask you or the instructor.

4. **Use an impartial but trained feedback facilitator when possible.**

   If possible, use an objective, trained feedback facilitator to gather the feedback so that students will feel comfortable criticizing the materials. Students are often reluctant to criticize a person's work when that person is physically present and looking at them face-to-face. Have an impartial facilitator

   - regularly solicit feedback about the effectiveness and quality of the course and course materials,

- ask clarifying and follow-up questions to accurately and fully capture the specifics of the feedback that is given,
- avoid justifying the existing state of the materials,
- avoid judging students' comments when they are made, and
- thank participants for their comments when they are made.

5. **Collect feedback from all course materials, not just the main lesson content.**

Measure the effectiveness of and gather feedback on all of the instructional materials, including exercises, labs, demonstrations, introductions, summaries, graphics, multimedia interactions, and the user interface (for technology-based training). Monitor how much time it takes students to complete these activities so you can adjust your stated student "seat times" in your topics or lessons.

6. **If significant changes are required as a result of the pilot, repeat the pilot again after you have made the changes.**

This is especially important when courses are developed with inadequate resources, attention, or time. A sculpture that is very rough will require more iterative chiseling and assessing than one that is already close to the final form.

Making Course Revisions

The next step in instructional development is to use the feedback gathered from the pilot and the review comments received from your reviewers to revise the course.

To revise your materials, follow these guidelines:

1. **Pay particular attention to content or issues for which several students had trouble.**

For example, if several students had trouble understanding a concept, you probably have a problem in the way you are teaching the concept.

2. **For issues for which only one or two students had trouble, perform a critical inspection of your materials.**

Just because only one or two students had trouble understanding something does not mean that you can just dismiss their experience outright. Look at your materials from an instructional design point of view. Did you fully employ the appropriate instructional strategy for the type of information being taught? Did you provide sufficient demonstrations and examples? Did you provide the opportunity for students to practice applying the information and receive feedback on their performance? Did you make any faulty assumptions about what students should already know? Even though students come from different backgrounds and experiences, you want *all* of your students from the target audience to achieve the course objectives.

3. **Budget in the beginning for time and resources to make the revisions.**

Making revisions requires time and staff to make those revisions, and the more technology and media elements that are used in the training, the more highly specialized professionals you will need, the longer it will take, and the more it will cost to make the changes. Because of this, budget early on in your project for sufficient time and resources to make the changes that are identified in the pilot.

4. **Provide for ongoing course feedback and suggestions and regular maintenance updates.**

After you have made the changes suggested by the pilot and your reviewers, provide an ongoing mechanism whereby future students can provide feedback about the course. This might be a simple feedback form that students can send in, a formal post-training course survey, or some other method. Provide periodic updates to the course that incorporate this feedback and bring the course content up to date.

5. **Remember that in creating a sculpture, chiseling away that last bit of rock is necessary to turn it into a masterpiece.**

Go the extra mile. Make the effort to perfect your course as much as you can before it goes out the door. Those final touches will go far in improving the course's perception by students and clients.

Publishing Your Course

Although not officially part of course development, the final act in creating a training course is to publish it, which is making it available for students to enroll and take. After you have piloted and revised your course and have received the final sign-off and permission from your client and other appropriate parties, you can then activate the course in the training delivery channel so that it is available for students to take.

The delivery channel might be something as sophisticated as a learning management system (LMS), which can handle student enrollments, course delivery (for technology delivered courses), and course management and administration. Or the delivery channel might be duplicating and distributing DVDs to individual students.

Some delivery channels can require several days from the time the final training deliverables or masters are delivered or uploaded until the course is officially available for students to take in the delivery channel. For example, an IT professional might have to enter certain information about the course into an LMS. To avoid unexpected delays, learn the business procedures in your organization for publishing courses in each delivery channel and include time in the project schedule to accommodate these requirements.

Chapter Summary—Piloting and Revising Course Materials

This chapter presented the final step in the instructional development process: how to conduct a pilot and revise the course based on the feedback gathered during the pilot.

You should now be able to

- define a course pilot and describe why it is important,
- describe why it is important to select students representatively in a pilot,
- describe why it is important to create a climate that is conducive for students to give feedback during the pilot,
- describe why you should solicit feedback at regular intervals during a pilot,
- describe why you should use an impartial but trained feedback facilitator when possible to gather feedback during a pilot,
- describe why you should gather feedback on all of the course materials during a pilot, not just on the main presentation content,
- describe when a pilot should be repeated,
- describe several guidelines on how to make revisions to your training materials based on a pilot of the materials, and
- describe several things you should anticipate and consider in publishing your course.

Check Your Understanding

1. **True or false? A course pilot is an early tryout of the course with anyone who is available to participate.**

2. **Piloting your training is important because it can help you: (Select all that apply.)**

    A. Demonstrate a return on investment.

    B. Publicize your course.

    C. Assess whether the training is effective and accomplished its objectives.

D. Create a favorable word-of-mouth reputation for the course.

E. Improve the training materials.

3. **True or false? In conducting a training pilot, selecting students representatively from the target audience means taking a purely random sample of students from the target audience.**

4. **True or false? Having an objective, third-party trained facilitator gather feedback during a pilot is usually more effective at getting honest, open feedback than having the training developer gather feedback because students will see a third-party facilitator as less vested in the training and less defensive about receiving feedback.**

5. **True or false? A course pilot should gather feedback on just the main presentation materials of the course.**

Answers

1. False. A course pilot is an early tryout of the course with representative students from the training audience in which student performance is assessed and student feedback is solicited both during and after the training.

2. C and E

3. False. Taking a purely random sample is rarely possible because you do not have a complete list of names of potential students of the course. Sampling students representatively means that you take a sample of students from each of the major audience subgroups that were identified during requirements, in direct proportion to that subgroup's percentage of the target audience. Suppose, for example, that you identified two audience subgroups, A and B, during requirements gathering, and subgroup A makes up 30% of the target audience and subgroup B makes up 70% of the target audience. Then for a pilot of ten students, you would solicit three students for the pilot from audience subgroup A and seven students from audience subgroup B.

4. True

5. False. A course pilot should gather feedback on all of the instructional events and activities of the course.

PART 2.

Developing Outstanding Slides, Screens, and Frames

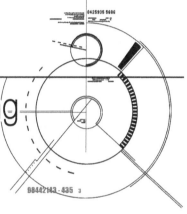

Overview of Part 2

Part 2 discusses how to create instructionally sound slides, screens, and frames—the smallest chunks of instruction that are presented at a time to students.

After you complete Part 2, you should be able to:

- List and explain the principles for creating effective titles for slides, screens, and frames.
- Define transitional slides, screens, and frames; explain their importance; and describe how they should be designed.
- List and describe sixteen principles for designing instructionally sound content for slides, screens, and frames.

Part two has 2 chapters.

Note: For detailed information on instructional design, see my companion book, *Instructional Design—Step by Step: Nine Easy Steps for Designing Lean, Effective, and Motivational Instruction.*

What Are Slides, Screens, and Frames?

Slides, screens, and frames are the smallest chunks of instruction that are presented at a time to students. Aside from presentations that involve continuous motion or animation, instruction must be broken up and presented in smaller, digestible chunks.

For example, as used in our discussion:

- For a slide presentation, a chunk is an individual *slide*.
- For a web-based training course, a chunk is an individual *screen*.
- For a hardcopy self-study training course, a chunk is a *page* (*frame*).

Why Is Slide, Screen, and Frame Design Important?

How these chunks of information are titled, transitioned from one slide to another, and laid out can greatly facilitate the student's understanding of the information that is presented.

Indeed, these decisions affect

- ease of sensory perception,
- ease of comprehension,
- retention,
- whether or not channel capacity is overloaded,
- the perception of information relevance,
- awareness of context during the course, and
- ease of future referencing of the material.

Is Crafting Decisions at This Level Worth the Effort?

In the push to develop the training and get it out the door, it is easy to think that you do not need to go down to this level of design or detail in developing your training materials.

However, professional educators firmly believe in the "magic" of this statement: The net result of making excellent design decisions at this level is far greater than the sum of the individual decisions.

The mark of a true professional is attention to details, not just to the overall design. In building a house, the final floor, wall, countertop, roofing, finish carpentry, trim work, and architectural details make a big difference in the overall feeling of quality, beauty, and design. Similarly, your attention to detail at this level makes a big difference in students' abilities to understand your training and use it after training for reference.

CHAPTER 10:
Creating Effective Slide Titles and Transitions

This chapter discusses how to create effective slide, screen, and frame titles and transitions.

What Are Titles and Why Are They Important?

Slide, screen, and frame titles are the words that label a chunk of information that is presented in its entirety—all at once or in a sequence of builds—to students. For example, titles label slides in slide shows, screens in web-based training, and frames or pages in hardcopy texts. Titles usually appear at the top of a slide, screen, or frame, although content can be broken down into subsections with subtitles that appear in the body of the text.

Titles provide a unique name for the small information chunk that is presented and serve several instructional purposes. Unfortunately, they are often given little attention or are poorly created, thereby hindering learning, comprehension, and ability of students to reference the training material at a later time.

Note: Throughout this chapter, to reduce verbiage, the term "slide" will often be used in place of "slide, screen, and frame." Also, to see a definition of instructional slides, screens, and frames, refer to the introduction to part 2 of this book.

Common Misconceptions about Slide Titles

Compare the following common misconceptions about titles with their truths:

Fiction: Slide titles should be as brief as possible.

Truth: They should be as brief as they can *and still fulfill their purpose*. It is more important for slides to fulfill their purpose than to be brief.

Fiction: Slide titles only need to state the general subject of the slide.

Truth: They should give students a clear and concise understanding of what information they can expect to see on the slide.

Fiction: Slide titles are not very important.

Truth: Titles provide several important instructional functions, including making transitions, providing an advanced organizer for the information, maintaining context, and setting expectations.

What Is the Purpose of Slide Titles?

Titles serve five distinct and important purposes. They:

1. Tell students exactly what *type* of information to expect on the slide.
2. Help provide and maintain *context* within the larger framework of the topic or lesson.
3. Reinforce the teaching strategy for the type of information being taught.

---

4. Flag transitions between major sections of content.

5. Facilitate the referencing of course information at a later time.

We will look at each of these purposes in detail in the remainder of this chapter.

Purpose #1. Titles Tell Students Exactly What Type of Information to Expect on the Slide

Titles serve as advanced organizers for the content that is on the slide. They set expectations for the information that will be presented. Therefore, titles should tell students *what* information they can expect to see on the slide.

Titles also give students an advanced organizer or summary statement about the type of information that they can expect on the slide. This advanced organizer assists students in their cognitive processing of the information on the slide.

Example of how slide titles can tell students what information to expect on a slide:

A poor example of a slide title would be "Firewalls." This title does not describe what specific type of information the student should expect to see on the slide. Will the slide discuss the definition of a firewall? Will it discuss the construction of a firewall? Will it discuss the administering a firewall? Or something entirely different? A student would not be able to tell.

A better example of a slide title would be "Using Firewalls to Enhance Network Security." This title tells students specifically what type of information to expect on the slide: how firewalls are used to enhance network security.

For more information on advanced organizers and human information processing, see Part 1, "Understanding How Humans Learn," in my companion book, *Instructional Design—Step by Step: Nine Easy Steps for Designing Lean, Effective, and Motivational Instruction*. Bloomington, IN: iUniverse, 2013.

How to Test a Title to See if It Identifies the Type of Information That Readers Expect to See on the Slide

To test a title that you have written to see if readers can tell the type of information to expect on a slide simply by reading its title, perform a *person-on-the-street test*:

> If you were to ask a person on the street or a person unfamiliar with the content to describe what type of information he or she would expect a slide to contain after hearing or reading its title, would that person correctly describe the specific type of information that the slide contains?

For example, consider the title, "How to test a title to see if it identifies the type of information that readers expect to see on the slide." From this title, would a person on the street or a person unfamiliar the topic know what type of information to expect on this slide simply by reading the title?

If you analyze this title, you will see that the answer is "yes." The phrase "how to" tells the student to expect to be taught a procedure or task. The title also tells a person *which* specific task will be taught; namely, how to see if a title tells readers the specific type of information that they can expect to see on this slide. Therefore, it passes the test.

The title "Partitioning" fails the person-on-the-street test. It does not tell a person what *specific* type of information to expect on the slide.

The title "How Partitions Enable Multiple Operating Systems to Exist on a Single Computer" passes the person-on-the-street test. It specifies the *specific* type of information that will be on the slide; namely, the process of how partitions allow multiple operating systems to exist on a single computer. Therefore, it passes the test.

Why the Person-on-the-Street Test Works

The person-on-the-street test works because it asks whether a person *who does not know the subject matter* can identify the specific type of information that will be presented on the slide, just by reading its title.

Subject matter experts already have elaborate mental constructs, rich mental networks, and detailed knowledge of the subject matter. Because of this, they often assume that students can infer meaning where they cannot. Slide titles must spell out the specific information that will appear on the slide because students are new to the subject area and do not yet possess these rich mental networks and constructs on which to draw.

Examples of Applying the Person-on-the-Street Test to Titles of Conceptual Information

Concepts are one of Robert Horn's seven types of information. Would the following titles for slides that teach concepts pass the person-on-the-street test?

Title #1

Mammals

This is a poor title. Compare it to the better titles below and read the explanation for why they are better.

Better title #1: Definition of a Mammal

Better title #2: What Are Mammals?

Explanation: "Mammals" is a concept. The title "Mammals" by itself is too broad and does not tell a person what specific aspects of mammals will be discussed on the slide.

Title #2

Clusters

This is a poor title. Compare it to the better titles below and read the explanation for why they are better.

Better title #1: Definition of a computer cluster

Better title #2: What is a computer cluster?

Explanation: "Computer clusters" is a concept. The title "Clusters" by itself is too broad and does not tell a person what specific information about clusters will be discussed on the slide. Will the slide present information on building a cluster, fixing a cluster, installing a cluster, selling clusters, or something entirely different? The student cannot tell.

Note: For more information on Horn's seven types of information, such as concepts and structures, which are used in the examples in this chapter, see chapter 3 in this book entitled, "Classifying Information into Its Type."

Examples of Applying the Person-on-the-Street Test to Titles of Structure-Type Information

Structures are another one of Horn's seven types of information. Would the following titles for slides that teach structures pass the person-on-the-street test?

Title #1

Stem Cells

This is a poor title. Compare it to the better titles below and read the explanation for why they are better.

Better title #1: Major Structures of Human Stem Cells

Better title #2: What Are the Major Structures of Human Stem Cells?

Explanation: The poor title identifies an object—stem cells—but provides no clues about what aspects of the stem cells will be discussed on the slide. The better titles provide definite clues about the type of information to expect on the slide.

Title #2

ZZ/T 1500I/O Bay

This is a poor title. Compare it to the better titles below and read the explanation for why they are better.

Better title #1: Components of the ZZ/T Model 1500 I/O Bay

Better title #2: What are the components of the ZZ/T Model 1500 I/O Bay?

Explanation: The poor title identifies an object—the Model 1500 I/O Boy—but provides no clues about what aspects of the Model 1500 I/O Bay will be discussed on the slide. The better titles provide definite clues about the type of information to expect on the slide.

Examples of Applying the Person-on-the-Street Test to Titles of Process Information

Processes are another one of Horn's seven types of information. Would the following titles for slides that teach processes pass the person-on-the-street test?

Title #1

Sod Production

This is a poor title. Compare it to the better titles below and read the explanation for why they are better.

Better title #1: How Sod Is Grown from Seed to Final Product

Better title #2: Growing Sod from Seed to Final Product

Explanation: The poor title is too broad. A person would not know which aspects of sod production will be presented on the slide. Is it the financial aspects, administrative aspects, caretaker aspects, or production aspects? The better titles provide definite clues as to what specific information to expect.

Title #2

Model ABC897 Data Flow

This is a poor title. Compare it to the better titles below and read the explanation for why they are better.

Better title #1: How Data Flows between the Model ABC897 and the Web server

Better title #2: Flow of Data between the Model ABC897 and the Web Server

Explanation: The poor title gives no clue as to what data flow is addressed. Is it between two internal entities, or between an internal and external entity?

Purpose #2. Titles Help Provide and Maintain Context within the Larger Framework of the Topic or Lesson

Slide titles help students maintain an awareness of larger context of where they are in the lesson and of how this particular slide relates back to the objectives of the lesson. To design titles that fulfill this purpose, follow these guidelines:

- **Create titles that relate to the overall organizing structure or framework that was introduced earlier in the lesson.**

For example, if an overview of a five steps of a task was given upfront in a lesson, then make it clear in the title of your slides which step you are discussing, such as "Step 2. Performing ..."

- **Create titles across slides that are in the same order and use the same or similar wording as was given in overview slides.**

  For example, for the objective, "Describe the key characteristics of the 2105 data recovery feature," an example title might be "Key Characteristics of the 2105 Data Recovery Feature."

- **Create sequences of titles across the slides in a lesson that collectively address the objective.**

  For example, for the objective, "Start a standard passenger car," example titles of the slides in the lesson might include, "Unlocking and Opening the Car Door," "Adjusting the Seat and Console," "Adjusting the Mirrors," "Fastening Your Safety Belt," and "Starting the Car."

- **Consider providing graphical clues** such as an icon or miniature version of an overview graphic that tie key slides back to a prior overview slide.

Purpose #3. Titles Reinforce the Teaching Strategy for the Type of Information Being Taught

If you use more than one slide to teach a procedure, process, principle, concept, fact, classification, or structure, then make the sequence of slide titles reflect the major teaching elements for that particular type of information.

For example, the strategy for teaching a concept includes defining the concept with its critical and variable attributes, providing examples and non-examples, and providing practice in classifying previously unencountered instances of the concept. The sequence of slide titles for the concept of a mammal might therefore be:

- Definition of Mammals
- Examples of Mammals
- Animals That Are Often Confused with Mammals [non-examples of mammals]
- Exercise: Which of the Following Are Mammals?

Example Sequence of Slide Titles for Teaching a Procedure

Suppose a lesson objective is: "Replace a defective disk drive in the Model ABC897 unit." This objective calls for the performance of a procedure, so the lesson will teach a procedure. One possible sequence of slide titles to teach this procedure is:

- Overview of Replacing a Defective Disk Drive
- Identifying the Location of the Disk Drive
- Setting the DIP Switches on the Model ABC897
- Step 1. Determine the Existing Drive Configuration
- Step 2. Shut Down the Computer and Disconnect the Power
- Step 3. Remove the Covers and the Defective Drive
- Step 4. Install and Configure the New Drive
- Step 5. Run Diagnostics on the New Drive
- Demonstration: Replacing a Defective Disk Drive
- Exercise: Replace a Defective Disk Drive

Example Sequence of Slide Titles for Teaching a Group of Related Concepts

Suppose a lesson objective is: "List the four types of network topologies, describe their attributes, and give two examples of each type of network." This objective calls for the student to demonstrate an understanding of four concepts (the four network topologies) so the lesson will teach a series of concepts. One possible sequence of slide titles to teach this group of related concepts is:

- The Four Major Types of Network Topologies
- Definition of Ring Network Topology
- Examples and Non-Examples of Ring Networks
- Checkpoint Questions: Which of the Following Are Ring Networks?
- Definition of Bus Network Topology
- Examples and Non-Examples of Bus Networks
- Checkpoint Questions: Which of the Following Are Bus Networks?
- Definition of Star Network Topology

- Examples and Non-Examples of Star Networks
- Checkpoint Questions: Which of the Following Are Star Networks?
- Definition of Star-Ring Network Topology
- Examples and Non-Examples of Star-Ring Topologies
- Checkpoint Question: Which of the Following Are Star-Ring Networks?
- Comparison of the Four Major Types of Network Topologies
- Integrative Exercise: Classifying Network Topologies

Example Sequence of Slide Titles for Teaching a Process

Suppose a lesson objective is: "Describe how an order is received and processed by the Order Fulfillment department." This objective calls for the student to demonstrate an understanding of a process, so the lesson will teach a process. One possible sequence of slide titles to teach this process is:

- Overview of the Order Fulfillment Process
- Phase 1. Receiving Orders
- Phase 2. Qualifying Orders
- Phase 3. Fulfilling Orders
- Phase 4. Shipping Orders
- Phase 5. Billing and Accounting for Orders

Purpose #4. Titles Flag Transitions between Major Sections of Content

Transitional slides are slides that help students transition from one subtopic to another or from one type of instructional activity to another. Transitions, for example, occur between one major section of the lesson and the next. In slide shows, for example, major sections of the presentation can be transitioned using transition slides, such as Part 1. [title of this section], Part 2. [title of this section], and so forth. The text or narration that accompanies these transition slides provides the mental bridge between one section and the next.

Another example of transitional slides is introductory and summary slides. These slides link a previous lesson to the current one or the current lesson to the next lesson, respectively.

Why transitional slides are important:

Without transitions, the cognitive thought and learning processes are rudely disrupted:

- Students need cues before their thought process are taken a new direction, just as drivers need to know about an upcoming fork or turn in the road.
- Without transitions, confusion, disjointedness, and disruption of learning can occur.

Students expect transitions, just as they do in ordinary conversation:

- "To change the subject ..."
- "Having seen what has happened in the past, what can we do in the future to ..."
- "Thanks, Mary, for your thoughts. Charlie, I would really like to hear your opinion on this now ..."
- "In contrast to what we have just discussed ..."
- "On the other hand, ..."
- "Notwithstanding what I have just said, ..."

Where Should You Place Transitional Slides?

Follow these guidelines in creating and placing transitional slides

- Always introduce (transition and overview) and close out (summarize and transition) major structural elements of the course, such as units and lessons or modules and topics.
- Provide transition slides anywhere a major shift in topic or content direction is made in the materials, or when there is a shift from one type of instructional activity to another (lecture to exercises, for example).
- For different types of transition slides (topic introduction, topic summary, checkpoint questions, exercises, demonstration, and so forth), use the

same design and layout for each type of transition slide. Make it easy for students to tell the type of transition slide just by its consistent appearance and layout. For example, use the same background graphic and slide layout on all checkpoint questions in the course.

Knowing where to create transition slides requires a sense of judgment, just as knowing where to provide transitions in everyday conversation does. Never cause the student to mentally stumble because you have suddenly made a transition without informing the student that you are doing so.

Purpose #5. Titles Facilitate the Referencing of Course Information at a Later Time

Students often return to their training materials after training to refresh their memories on a task or to look up information. Will your slide titles make it easy for students to find the information that they are looking for?

In some courses, for example, the individual slide titles are included in a detailed table of contents for the course. Are your titles written so that students can quickly scan them to find the very slide that contains the information that they are seeking?

Even if a detailed table of contents is not provided, well-crafted titles can help students scan through the course materials and quickly identify the location of detailed information. If titles are too short or too broad in meaning, students will have to sort through the detailed content of many slides to find the information that they are seeking. Titles that tell students what information to expect on the slide make it easy to find detailed information just by scanning the slide titles.

An example of how slide titles can help or hinder the ability of students to reference course information:

Compare the two columns of slide titles in the following table for a course lesson entitled, "Problem Determination for Control Workstations."

Poor slide titles	Better slide titles
CWS	What Is the Control Workstation (CWS)?
Documentation and support	When to Use the MAPS Manuals and Call Centers
	Overview of How to Perform CWS Problem Determination
ERRLG.log	1. Check the CWS Error Log for Error Messages
SysInfo	2. Use the SysInfo Command to Query for CWS Errors
BckupImage	3. Check the Image Backup File for Errors
EventLog	4. Set Up an Event Monitoring Log
Ping	5. Use the Ping Command to Query CWS Communications
Cabling	6. Check for Proper Cabling

The more informative slide titles enable students to determine if the information that they are seeking can be found on a particular slide. The poor slide titles fail to do this unless students are looking for any information related to the one or two words used in the title. Even then, students still do not know if the particular aspect of the topic that they are interested in is covered on that slide. For example, the ping command can be used for other things besides querying CWS communications.

Chapter Summary—Creating Effective Slide Titles and Transitions

This chapter discussed how to create effective slide, screen, and frame titles and transitions.

You should now be able to

- define slide titles and explain why they are important;
- describe several misconceptions about slide titles;
- list the five purposes of slide titles and, for each purpose, explain it, state why it is important to fulfill, and provide several examples of titles that do and do not fulfill that purpose:
    1. Tell students exactly what type of information to expect on the slide.
    2. Help provide and maintain context within the larger framework of the topic or lesson.
    3. Reinforce the teaching strategy for the type of information being taught.
    4. Flag transitions between major sections of content.
    5. Facilitate the referencing of course information at a later time.
- describe how to test a title to see if it identifies the type of information to expect on the slide;
- explain why the person-on-the-street test of a slide title works;
- provide examples of applying the person-on-the-street test to titles of conceptual information;
- provide examples of applying the person-on-the-street test to titles of structure information;
- provide examples of applying the person-on-the-street test to titles of process information;
- provide example sequences of slide titles for teaching a concept;
- provide example sequences of slide titles for teaching a procedure;
- provide example sequences of slide titles for teaching a group of related concepts;

- provide example sequences of slide titles for teaching a process;
- define transitional slides; and
- describe where you should place transitional slides.

Check Your Understanding

1. **True or false? In making revisions to your course based on a pilot, you can ignore changing your materials if only one or two students had trouble with a particular issue.**

2. **Publishing a course before you make any of the changes suggested by the course pilot can: (Select all that apply.)**
    A. Alter your client's view of your training abilities.
    B. Satisfy your client in the long run.
    C. Mar your professional reputation.
    D. Frustrate students who subsequently take the course.
    E. Impress others with your ability to beat deadlines.

3. **True or false? Publishing a course—making it available for students to enroll and take after course development is complete—typically requires some time to accomplish.**

4. **True or false? Slide, screen, and frame titles are of minor importance to learning compared to the main course content.**

5. **Which of the following statements about slide titles are true? (Select all that apply.)**
    A. It is more important for slides to fulfill their purpose than to be brief.
    B. They are not very important.
    C. They should give students a clear and concise understanding of what information they can expect to see on the slide.
    D. They only need to state the subject of the slide.
    E. They should be as brief as possible.
    F. They provide several important instructional functions.

6. **The purpose of slide titles is to: (Select all that apply.)**
    A. Facilitate the referencing of course information at a later time.

B. Reinforce the teaching strategy for the type of information being taught.

C. Help provide and maintain context within the larger framework of the topic or lesson.

D. Create a cryptic but accurate title for the slide.

E. Flag transitions between major sections of content.

F. Tell students exactly what type of information to expect on the slide.

7. **True or false? Slide, screen, and frame titles serve as advanced organizers for the content that is on the slide.**

8. **The person-on-the-street-test for slide titles asks a hypothetical person on the street or a person who is unfamiliar with the subject matter to: (Select all that apply.)**

A. Create a title for a slide, given the slide contents.

B. Give their opinion as to whether or not they like a slide title.

C. Answer a question about a specific piece of content on a slide after hearing or reading its title.

D. Describe what type of information he or she would expect a slide to contain after hearing or reading its title.

E. Critique a title for a slide after hearing or reading the title and comparing it to the contents of the slide.

9. **True or false? The person-on-the-street test works because it asks whether a person who knows the subject matter can identify the specific type of information that will be presented on the slide, just by reading its title.**

10. **Classify each of the following slide titles as poor or good:**

A. How to Format a Model ZYX321 Disk Drive

B. Tips for Communicating with Your Teenager

C. The TTZY-125 Copy Machine

D. Safety

E. What is Ohm's law?

F. Extracting More Joules from the Crypto Unit

G. Specifications

H. Overview of How Plywood Is Made

I. Component Parts of a Sailboat Rig

11. **In creating slide titles, to help students maintain context and know where they are at within the larger framework of the topic or lesson, you should: (Select all that apply.)**

    A. Consider providing graphical clues such as an icon or miniature version of an overview graphic that tie key slides back to a prior overview slide.

    B. Create titles across slides that are in the same order and use the same or similar wording as was given in overview slides.

    C. Create sequences of titles across the slides in a lesson that collectively address the objective.

    D. Ask your subject matter experts to create the slide titles.

    E. Create titles that relate to the overall organizing structure or framework that was introduced earlier in the lesson.

12. **How can a sequence of slide, screen, and frame titles reinforce the teaching strategy for the type of information being taught? (Select all that apply.)**

    A. The titles can be constructed to provide good summaries of the content on each slide.

    B. The titles can be worded to signal transitions in the sections of the topic.

    C. The titles can emphasize the key information on each slide.

    D. The titles can reflect the major teaching elements for that particular type of information.

    E. The titles can be worded in a friendly and conversational way.

13. **True or false? The following sequence of slide titles is appropriate for teaching the concept of a Widget.**
    - Definition of Widgets
    - Examples of Widgets
    - Examples of Things That Are Not Widgets
    - Exercise: Which of the Following Are Widgets?

14. **True or false? The following sequence of slide titles is appropriate for teaching the procedure for making a cake.**
    - Overview of Making a Cake
    - How Cakes Rise
    - Phase 1. How Oven Controls Work
    - Phase 1. Ingredients Are Assembled
    - Phase 2. Ingredients Are Mixed
    - Phase 3. Mix Is Placed in a Baking Pan
    - Phase 4. Mix Is Baked
    - Phase 5. Cake Is Cooled and Removed

15. **True or false? The following sequence of slide titles is appropriate for teaching the process of how milk is turned into butter at a processing plant.**
    - Overview of How Milk Is Turned into Butter
    - Phase 1. Milk Is Received at the Receiving Dock
    - Phase 2. Milk Cream Is Separated from the Milk
    - Phase 1. Milk Cream Is Pumped into Mechanical Churns
    - Phase 2. Cream Is Churned until It Becomes Butter
    - Phase 3. Butter Is Removed and Injected into Forms
    - Phase 4. Butter Is Cooled and Packaged
    - Phase 5. Butter Is Quality Tested
    - Phase 6. Butter Is Shipped
    - Activity: Video of How Butter Is Made
    - Quiz: How Butter Is Made

16. **Why are transitional slides, screens, and frames important? (Select all that apply.)**
    A. Transitional slides help break up the monotony of a long string of slides.
    B. Students need cues that their thought process is going to be taking a new direction, just as drivers need to know there is an upcoming fork or turn in the road.
    C. Without transitions, confusion, temporary disjointedness, and temporary halting of learning can occur.
    D. Students expect transitions, just as they do in ordinary conversation.

E. Transitional slides provide additional content that makes the course appear more substantial.

17. **True or false? Transitional slides, screens, and frames are typically used to (1) introduce and close out major structural chunks of the course, such as units and lessons, (2) to transition from one major topic of discussion to another within a lesson, (3) and to transition from one type of instructional activity to another.**

18. **Why do titles for slides, screens, or frames that are too short or too broad in meaning make it difficult for students to reference the course materials after training?**
    A. Students will have to look at the slides before and after to determine if a slide has the information that they are seeking.
    B. Students will have to contact the course owners to know where the information that they are seeking can be found.
    C. Students will be forced to read and sort through the detailed content of many slides to determine if they contain the particular information that they are seeking.
    D. Students will have to contact the subject matter experts to know where the information that they are seeking can be found.

Answers

1. False. Students have different backgrounds and abilities. You want *all* of your students from the target audience to successfully achieve the course objectives. Moreover, some students are more perceptive to learning issues and can identify problems that other students cannot see or articulate.
2. A, C, and D
3. True. Depending on the complexity of the delivery channel, publishing can itself take one or more days to accomplish. Sometimes specific IT-oriented professionals have to perform certain actions in the LMS to integrate the course into the system. You might also have to obtain permission to publish the course from the business owner of the area for which training is being provided. Learn what the procedures are in your

organization and build time into the project schedule to accommodate these requirements.

4. False. Slide titles are very important to learning, comprehension, and ability of students to reference the training material at a later time.

5. A, C, and F

6. A, B, C, E, and F

7. True. It gives students an advanced organizer and a mental "warning" about the type of information to come. This assists in cognitive processing.

8. D

9. False. The person-on-the-street test works because it asks whether a person *who does not know the subject matter* can identify the specific type of information that will be presented on the slide, just by reading its title.

10. A, good title; B, good title; C, poor title; D, poor title; E, good title; F, good title; G, poor title; H, good title; and I, good title. Titles C, D, and G are too broad. What specific aspects of these topics will be discussed?

11. A, B, C, and E

12. D

13. True

14. False. The following would be a more appropriate sequence of slides because they reflect the major instructional elements for teaching procedures:
    - Overview of Baking a Cake
    - How to Measure Ingredients
    - Step 1. Pre-Heat the Oven
    - Step 2. Assemble the Ingredients
    - Step 3. Mix the Ingredients
    - Step 4. Place the Mix into a Baking Pan
    - Step 5. Bake the Cake
    - Step 6. Cool the Cake and Remove It from the Pan
    - Demonstration: Making a Cake
    - Exercise: Make a Cake

15. True. The sequence of slides reflects the major instructional elements for teaching procedures.
16. B, C, and D
17. True
18. C

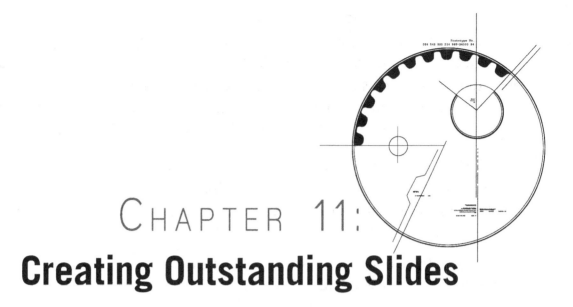

CHAPTER 11:
Creating Outstanding Slides

The last chapter focused on slide titles and transition slides. This chapter discusses sixteen principles for creating outstanding slides, screens, and frames. This chapter focuses on the content on the slide, not its title.

Why Slide Design Is Important

Designing the content of slides is just as important as creating good slide titles. Every hindrance, confusion, and cognitive stumbling block that students encounter in the body of a slide consumes their limited mental resources, hinders comprehension, and slows learning.

Although an occasional inadvertent bit of confusion may seem trivial, the cumulative effect of many instances of confusion—whether unintentional or created out of ignorance of good design—is profound. Even one bit of confusion can be a showstopper if it is about a critical prerequisite concept or skill. You must learn to walk before you learn to run.

One of the responsibilities of an instructional developer is to design the layout, structure, and presentation of content at the level of the actual instructional materials, which includes all of the instructional presentations, exercises, and activities. Part 1 of this book discussed specific development principles in the context of the instructional development process. This chapter discusses sixteen general principles of slide design that stand on their own.

Note: Throughout this chapter, to reduce verbiage, the term "slide" will often be used in place of "slide, screen, and frame." Also, to see a definition of instructional slides, screens, and frames, refer to the introduction for part 2.

Principle #1. Chunk Course Content into Unified, Single-Purpose Slides

Slides are a physical and logical partitioning of the course content into informational chunks. In a sense, they are the smallest sequences for learning that are presented to the student as a whole.

In chunking course content into unified, single-purpose slides:

- Make each slide represent a logical, cohesive, unified chunk of information. This means that each slide should have one well-defined theme or topic of discussion, as set forth by the slide title.
- Avoid major changes in topic or theme within a slide. Instead, make these changes across slides, and for large changes, use transitional slides to set off a new section or topic of discussion.

Principle #2. Avoid Overloading Slides with Too Much Content or Detail

Students learn best when instruction is presented in relatively small, unified chunks, each of which supports a clear and single purpose. Some slide designers try to cram as much information as possible into every slide, creating densely packed slides of text and complex graphics. Remember, your slides are not individual advertisements that are being placed in a newspaper that charges by the area of the ad, so avoid overloading your slides with too much content or detail.

To avoid overloading slides with too much content:

- Divide large bodies of content into logical subparts and create separate slides for each of the subparts.
- If all of the key or essential content cannot be placed on a single slide, chunk the content across multiple slides. For the other slides, consider using the same slide title with "(1 of x)" appended on the end of the title.
- Place nice-to-know information in appendices or point to it by reference or with links.

Principle #3. Layer Information both Verbally and Visually

Layering information is a key learning principle. Students learn best when they are first presented with a high-level structure or overview information and then with detailed information thereafter, using the overview to provide context and structure.

To layer information:

- Layer information not only visually, but verbally.
- Place the most important, key, or high-level information in the top layer.
- Use slide titles and other layering mechanisms. Slide titles provide the first level of overview for the content on a slide, but other mechanisms can also be used to layer slide content, including header levels, indentation, hierarchy, typography, emphasis, bullet lists, white space, callout boxes, sidebars, and colored backgrounds.
- Check to see if your content is layered in your presentation. For example, scan each slide visually to see if the most important and key information stands out.
- Layer complex information across several slides, placing more detailed information in subsequent slides.

For additional information on layering, see the two chapters on "Twenty Common Training Mistakes," in part 3 in my companion book, *Instructional Design— Step by Step: Nine Easy Steps for Designing Lean, Effective, and Motivational Instruction*. Bloomington, IN: iUniverse, 2013.

Principle #4. Emphasize Key Content

Another key teaching principle is to emphasize key information in the slide.

Key information is information that meets at least one of the following criteria:

- Foundational information on which other important information is based
- Information that greatly facilitates, organizes, or simplifies the understanding of other information
- Information that must be understood to learn other important information
- Information that will be needed by the student to produce important job outcomes

Key information includes the key principles for a subject area and the key steps and performance guidance for a procedure.

To emphasize key content:

- Draw students' attention visually and verbally to that which is most important on the slide.
- Use visual techniques for emphasizing information including type size, indention, white space, arrows, boxes, bolding, color, encircling, callouts, and so forth.

- Use verbal techniques for emphasizing information including pointing out key information in the text narrative itself, referring to it repeatedly, and giving it more discussion and explanation.
- Test your slide for proper emphasis of key information by asking yourself, "Does the most important, key information receive the greatest emphasis both visually and verbally on this slide?"

Principle #5. Create Headers or Bullet List Entries That Support the Slide Title

For example, the highest level of headers or bullet points in a slide show should directly support the purpose conveyed by the slide title.

To support the slide title with your headers or bullet points:

- Make the highest-level headers or bullet points on a slide consistent with the slide title. If the title says, "Example of ...", then the headers should *not* say "Principle #1," "Principle #2," and so forth.
- Test the top-level entries on your slide against the slide title to see if they support the title. Scan the headers or bullet points and see if they directly address the expected type of information as conveyed by the slide title.

Examples of bullet lists that do and do not support the slide title:

Good example: For a slide entitled, "Advantages of HTML," bullet list entries supporting the slide title would be:

- Small file size
- Faster transmission across the network
- Portability across different hardware and software platforms
- Easy to learn

Poor example: For a slide entitled, "Ways to Improve System Security," bullet list entries that do *not* support the slide title would be:

- Security is a major system issue
- Major security vendors
- Routers and firewalls
- Encryption issues

- Internet security protocols

The title in the poor example creates the expectation that a list of entries beginning with verbs will follow, such as "Add a firewall," "Use SSL encryption," and "Add an intelligent router." Moreover, this slide is not unified. Furthermore, the first, second, and last bullets do not even belong on this slide.

Principle #6. Make Sure That All Slide Content Supports the Purpose Set Forth by the Title

This principle is one of the most frequently violated principles of slide design. Slide content can easily drift away from the strict purpose of the slide, as set forth by the title, unless you are careful and disciplined.

To follow this principle:

- Eliminate any content that does not support the clear and singular purpose of the slide. The purpose of a slide, for example, might be to present a concept or principle, give an overview, present a set of related facts, or give a step in a procedure.
- In populating the slide with content, be true to the purpose of the slide.
- Each slide should have only one singular purpose. All content should support that purpose. Create additional slides for content that does not fit into this singular purpose.

Principle #7. Use Parallel Structure in Bullet List Entries

Parallel structure in a list means using the same grammatical construction for each entry in the list.

For example, consider a slide entitled, "How to Improve Your Health." Compare the non-parallel and parallel list entries in the following table:

Non-parallel entries	Parallel entries
It is important to eat a healthy diet.	Eat healthy food.
You should exercise aerobically four or five times a week for at least 30 minutes.	Exercise aerobically most days for at least 30 minutes.
Working out with weights will build muscle which helps burn fat.	Work out with weights three or four times a week.
Daily stretching is also good for you.	Perform stretching exercises every day.
Studies have shown that exposure to environmental pollutants over a lifetime is hazardous to your health.	Avoid exposure to environmental pollutants.
"Cleanliness is next to godliness."	Practice proper hygiene.
Do not be around those who are ill.	Avoid exposure to those with contagious illnesses.
Stress can kill.	Manage stress.

Notice that the parallel entries all have the same grammatical construction: They all begin with a verb. The non-parallel entries do not.

Principle #8. Apply the Principle of Contiguity to Group-Related Information

Contiguity refers to the phenomenon that humans infer that two objects or ideas are related if they are placed close together in time or space.

Examples of contiguity in time include expecting that the next sentence that you hear is related to the previous one or that the next slide that is presented is related to the previous slide.

Examples of contiguity in space include making the assumption that items that are grouped close together are somehow related to each other, assuming that a text label next to a callout line in a graphic is the label associated with the object to which the line is drawn, or that sentences within "blocks" of text are related to each other.

People often assign causality to events that occur close in time. For example, if a mother honks a car horn and her daughter comes out of the house shortly thereafter, the mother is probably forming a causal relationship that honking the horn speeds up the appearance of her daughter in front of the house.

How this principle is applied to slide design:

For contiguity in time: In a presentation, students expect that the next slide's content will be related to the previous slide's content unless told otherwise. They also expect that the next sentence that an instructor speaks will be related to the previous one unless told otherwise.

For contiguity in space: On a slide, place related content physically close to each other on the slide and farther away from other content. For example, compare the two layouts in the following table:

The following table shows an example of good and bad use of the continuity of space:

Poor use of contiguity of space	Better use of contiguity of space

• Bejk aone ocid jeokse
   • Poiwed iod qiodov
 	
   • Pointra zod kwerlk
• Yowg iox roenp qir von
 	
   • Yocv bweax mnirp
   • Zwracp pibnw comw
   • Uiz muortc pow yrut
	• Bejk aone ocid jeokse
	   • Poiwed iod qiodov
	   • Pointra zod kwerlk
	
	• Yowg iox roenp qir von
	   • Yocv bweax mnirp
	   • Zwracp pibnw comw
	   • Uiz muortc pow yrut

The layout in the rightmost column leads a person to believe that the text within each of the two groups is somehow related to each other because the text is close together physically and farther away from other text.

Principle #9. Avoid Creating Mysterious Information

Avoid presenting information that leaves students permanently puzzled over the meaning of that information. To avoid creating mysterious information:

- Make slides as self-explanatory as possible.
- Avoid using your own, nonstandard abbreviations on graphics or tables.
- If you use acronyms, technical terms, or abbreviations in graphics or tables, provide a key on the graphic or table or in the accompanying text.
- Always define new terms when they are used on a slide.
- Eliminate technical details and terms that are not necessary for the purpose at hand.

Principle #10. Be Consistent Within and Across Slides

Inconsistencies slow students down and require that they decode yet another information mystery or cognitive puzzle.

To be consistent within and across slides:

- Strive for consistency in everything. For example, if you are teaching a procedure that requires multiple slides, be consistent in how you word and present the titles, graphics, step instructions, step feedback, and other information.
- For technology-based training, be consistent in the design and function of user interface and navigation elements.
- Create and follow a set of style guidelines in developing your training to help ensure consistency across slides.

Principle #11. Strive for Visual Balance on Slides

Visual balance is achieved when the visual elements on the slide would balance if they had weight in proportion to their size and density and were placed on an imaginary horizontal board with the fulcrum in the center.

Compare the following two visual presentations:

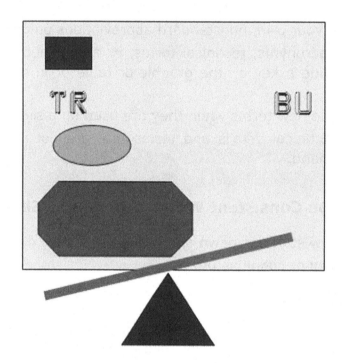

Figure 7. An unbalanced visual presentation

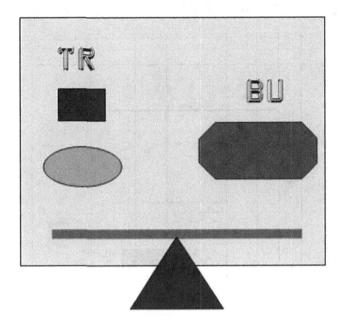

Figure 8. A balanced visual presentation

To achieve visual balance, place the elements of the presentation so that they would balance.

Principle #12. Minimize the Number of Vertical Alignment Lines

Vertical alignment lines are imaginary vertical lines that line up with the edge of one or more objects on the slide.

To follow this principle, avoid an unnecessary number of vertical alignment lines. Generally, a smaller number of lines is better.

Compare the following two visual presentations:

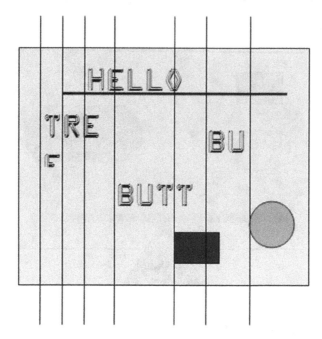

Figure 9. Too many unnecessary vertical alignment lines

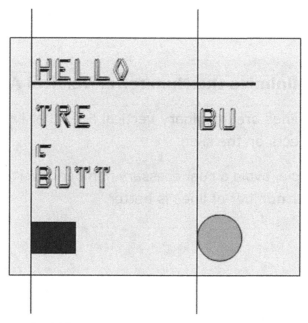

**Figure 10. Objects rearranged to have a minimum
number of vertical alignment lines**

Principle #13. Choose a Type Size That Is Appropriate for the Presentation Technology

Students must be able to easily read the information that is presented to them. Older students might need larger type sizes to read text comfortably.

For slides that are projected onto a screen (for example, in front of a classroom):

- Generally, a type size of 24 to 46 points in the slide is sufficient to enable students at the back of the classroom to read the text. **Note:** Points is a unit of measurement: 72 points = 1 inch.
- Before going live with your training, check the projected image size using the actual classroom equipment as many factors affect the size of a projected image, including the lens in the projector.

For text that is displayed on a computer screen or other electronic screen, as a general rule, use text that is 10 to 12 points or larger.

Principle #14. Strive for Greater Organization

To organize your content, use tables, columns, white space, and other methods to add meaningful organization to a slide.

A table, for example, is a powerful way of organizing and presenting a comparison:

Before the World-Wide Web	After the World-Wide Web
Text only	Graphics on web pages
Some technical expertise required by end users to use efficiently	Little or no technical expertise required by end users
Text commands	Graphical browsers

Principle #15. Strive for Simplicity and Conciseness

To follow this principle:

- Write simple, concise text.

- At the same time, avoid being cryptic or incomplete.
- Leave out any unnecessary elements.

As one researcher that we previously referenced, Ruth Clark, pointed out in her *Coherence Principle,* that adding interesting material can actually *hurt* learning.

Examples of interesting but unnecessary material include adding unnecessary stories, background music and sounds, or interesting but extraneous graphics. According to Clark, these unnecessary additions can hinder learning through the following three mechanisms:

- Distraction: Diverting attention away
- Disruption: Preventing correct associations from being made
- Seduction: Priming inappropriate knowledge

Principle #16. Flip Back and Forth between the Previous Slides and the Current Slide

When cartoon animators create animations by hand, they flip back and forth between their current sketch and their prior ones to see if the animation flows smoothly, without any abrupt jumps or breaks in continuity.

To implement this principle, do the same with your slides:

- Page back and forth between the current slide and the previous ones.
- Ask yourself the following questions:
  - Does the current slide flow logically from previous slides, especially the previous one?
  - Does the current slide's title flow from and fit in with the previous slide titles?
  - Does the current slide fit in with the overviews, structures, and expectations that I set up in a previous or introductory slide?

Chapter Summary —Creating Outstanding Slides

This chapter discussed sixteen principles for creating outstanding slides, screens, and frames. This chapter focused on the content on the slide, not its title.

You should now be able to

- explain why slide, screen, and frame design is important to learning; and
- for each of the following sixteen principles of slide, screen, and frame design, define the principle, explain how it can be applied, and provide examples and non-examples of its application:
  - Chunk course content into unified, single-purpose slides.
  - Avoid overloading slides with too much content or detail.
  - Layer information both verbally and visually.
  - Emphasize key content.
  - Create headers or bullet list entries that support the slide title.
  - Make sure that all slide content supports the purpose set forth by the title.
  - Use parallel structure in bullet list entries.
  - Apply the principle of contiguity to group related information.
  - Avoid creating mysterious information.
  - Be consistent within and across slides.
  - Strive for visual balance on slides.
  - Minimize the number of vertical alignment lines.
  - Choose a type size that is appropriate for the presentation technology.
  - Strive for greater organization.
  - Strive for simplicity and conciseness.
  - Flip back and forth between the previous slides and the current slide.

Check Your Understanding

1. **True or false? The design of slide, screen, or frame content can impact comprehension and learning just as much as creating good slide titles.**

2. **True or false? An individual slide, screen, or frame should fulfill as many purposes and provide as much content as you have room on the slide, screen, or frame.**

3. **True or false? Slides, screens, and frames that are densely packed with information are better than slides, screens, and frames that have less information because students can see more information at one time and relate the information together.**

4. **True or false? Information on a slide, screen, or frame can be layered using techniques that employ slide titles, header levels, indentation, hierarchy, typography, emphasis, bullet lists, white space, callout boxes, sidebars, and colored backgrounds.**

5. **Verbally pointing out key information in the main body of a slide, screen, or frame, referring to that key information repeatedly, and giving it more discussion and explanation are examples of ____ techniques for emphasizing information.**

6. **True or false? Information on a slide, screen, or frame can be layered using techniques that employ slide titles, header levels, indentation, hierarchy, typography, emphasis, bullet lists, white space, callout boxes, sidebars, and colored backgrounds.**

7. **True or false? It is acceptable for slide, screen, or frame content to fulfill other purposes other than that which is conveyed by the slide title.**

8. **What is wrong with the following bullet list for a slide or screen entitled, "How to Make Work More Enjoyable?"**
    - It is important to get a good night's rest.
    - You should eat a good breakfast.
    - Praise the boss's taste in clothing.
    - Taking frequent two-minute breaks adds more enjoyment to your day.
        A. Some of the entries fail to support the purpose of the slide.
        B. It is not written concisely.
        C. It is too informal in style.
        D. The list items do not use parallel structure.
        E. It is not in the right order.

9. True or false? Continuity refers to the phenomenon that humans tend to think that two things are related if they are placed close together in time or space.

10. True or false? Examples of putting mysterious information on your slides, screens, and frames include using unknown acronyms or labels; including graphics or tables that use your own, nonstandard abbreviations; and using undefined acronyms and technical terms.

11. True or false? The principle of consistency applies not only within slides and screens, but across slides and screens and across the entire course.

12. True or false? Visual balance in a slide or screen is achieved when 80% or more of viewers judge the slide to be visually pleasing.

13. True or false? Vertical alignment lines are imaginary vertical lines that line up with the edge of one or more objects on a slide, screen, or frame.

14. True or false? For slides that are projected in front of a classroom of students, a type size of 24 to 46 points is usually sufficient to enable students at the back of the classroom to read the text.

15. True or false? To achieve greater organization of information on a slide, screen, or frame, use tables, columns, white space, and other techniques to organize the information.

16. True or false? According to Ruth Clark's Coherence Principle, adding interesting material to your training presentations, such as background music and sounds, increases learning.

17. In developing slides, screens, and frames, why should you flip back and forth between previous slides, screens, or frames and the current one? (Select all that apply.)
    A. To see if the current slide summarizes the content of the previous slides
    B. To see if this slide fits in with the overviews, structures, and expectations that you set up in a previous or introductory slide
    C. To see if this slide's title flows from and fits in with the previous slide titles

D. To see if you put too much information on the current slide

E. To see if the current slide flows logically from the previous slides

Answers

1. True

2. False. Each slide should have one well-defined theme or topic of discussion, as set forth by the slide title.

3. False. You should avoid overloading slides with too much content or detail.

4. True

5. The correct answer is "verbal."

6. True

7. False. All slide content should support the purpose set forth by the title.

8. D

9. False. *Contiguity*, not continuity (check the spelling of the two terms carefully and notice the difference), refers to the phenomenon that people tend to think that two things are related if they are placed close together in time or space.

10. True

11. True

12. False. *Visual balance* is achieved when the visual elements on the slide would balance if they had weight in proportion to their size and density and were placed on an imaginary horizontal board with the fulcrum in the center.

13. True

14. True

15. True

16. False. According to Clark, these unnecessary additions can *hinder* learning through the following three mechanisms:

   • Distraction: Diverting attention away

   • Disruption: Preventing correct associations from being made

   • Seduction: Priming inappropriate knowledge

17. B, C, and E

Summary

Congratulations! You have now completed the instructional part of this book. You should now be able to

- define instructional development and explain how it is a continuation and refinement of the instructional design;
- given an instructional design document, create (write or author) the final course presentations, activities, and other deliverables by following the six steps of instructional development:
    1. Perform an analysis of the objectives to determine all enabling content.
    2. Classify information into its type and create corresponding instructional presentations.
    3. Create the remaining instructional events and finalize the topic.
    4. Create scripts (for technology-based training).
    5. Perform a quality check on the training materials.
    6. Pilot and revise all course materials.
- list and explain the principles for creating effective titles for slides, screens, and frames;
- define transitional slides, screens, and frames; explain their importance; and describe how they should be designed; and
- list and describe sixteen principles for creating outstanding slides, screens, and frames.

You should now be better prepared to create effective, lean, and motivational training.

What You Should Have Learned

In part 1, you learned the six major steps of instructional development; how to perform an analysis of the objectives to determine all enabling content; how to classify information into its type; how to design information presentations that match the information's type; how to create instructional events; how to finalize lessons and topics; and how to validate, quality check, pilot, and revise course materials.

In part 2, you learned how to create instructionally sound slides, screens, and frames—the smallest chunks of instruction that are presented at a time to students. More specifically, you learned several principles for creating effective titles for slides, screens, and frames; how and where to create transitional slides, screens, and frames; and sixteen principles for designing, laying out, and structuring content for slides, screens, and frames.

Your Next Steps

This book discussed the fundamental concepts, processes, and procedures of sound instructional development. Hopefully, you found it easy to understand, logically sequenced, and relevant to your own personal needs. It presented many activities, examples, and questions with feedback to help you learn this information.

However, this book can only take you so far. Now that you have been grounded in the fundamentals of instructional development, your next step is to apply your knowledge and skills to the real world. Hopefully, you will do this under the tutelage of an experienced instructional developer who has a deep understanding of this process. By doing so, you can continue to learn and refine your abilities through further practice with feedback on actual projects.

Therefore, seek out a mentor who can provide that feedback and help you improve your skills.

And, if you have not already read my companion book, *Instructional Design—Step by Step: Nine Easy Steps for Designing Lean, Effective, and Motivational Instruction,* please do so. Instructional development is a continuation of the instructional design that was created by the instructional designer. Knowing the fundamental principles of learning and design will help you become a more professional instructional developer.

Appendix A: A Partial Example of a Script for a Topic in a Web-based Training Course

Script for Module 1, Topic 1: Overview of How to Develop Training

Module 1: Topic 1	Event Type and Description: Topic Introduction	**Screen # 1**

Event Graphic(s): Standard topic introduction/background.

Event Text:

Topic Introduction – Overview of How to Develop Training

This topic presents an overview of the instructional development process. It describes the major activities involved in developing training, including analyzing topic objectives to determine all of the enabling content for a topic; classifying information into its type; designing information presentations that match the information's type; creating exercises and other instructional events; finalizing the sequence of materials for a topic; creating scripts for technology-based training; performing a quality check on the training materials; and piloting and revising the course materials.

After you complete this topic, you should be able to

- list the six steps of the instructional development process;
- for each of the following steps in the development process, state the purpose of that step, describe how it is carried out at a high level, and explain why that step is important:
  - Analyze the objectives to determine all enabling content.
  - Classify information into its type and create corresponding instructional presentations.
  - Create the remaining instructional events and finalize the topic.
  - Create scripts (for technology-based training).

- Perform a quality check on the training materials.
- Pilot and revise all course materials, and
- describe how instructional development is a continuation and refinement of the instructional design.

This topic takes approximately 35 minutes to complete.

Click Next to continue.

Module 1: Topic 1	Event Type and Description: Text with graphic with hotspot that pops up text	**Screen # 2**

Event Graphic(s): Graphic of a six-step process for instructional development (see a similar graphic in Mod 2, Topic 1, screen 2 or 3 of the other course). The six steps to include in the graphic are:

1. Analyze the objectives to determine all enabling content [placing the cursor over this step displays the following pop up: Analyze the objectives to determine each objective's type (skill, knowledge, or attitude); then, complete the analysis of the objective using the analysis techniques appropriate for that type of objective. This results in a collection of all of the enabling content that must be taught for that objective. Repeat these steps for each objective in the course.

2. Classify information into its type and create corresponding instructional presentations [placing the cursor over this step displays the following pop up text: For each type of enabling content, create the presentational material following the instructional strategy that is appropriate for teaching that information type.]

3. Create the remaining instructional events and finalize the topic [placing the cursor over this step displays the following pop up text: Create the exercises and other instructional events specified in the instructional design document, determine if any additional prerequisite information needs to be refreshed, and determine the overall sequence of all presentation and instructional events for the topic.]

4. Create scripts (for technology-based training) [placing the cursor over this step displays the following pop up text: Create scripts that specify all necessary text and design elements for a technology specialist in the delivery technology to create the instructional presentation or event.]

5. Perform a quality check on the training materials [placing the cursor over this step displays the following pop up text:] Perform a review to ensure that the content supports the objectives (no extraneous content) and that all objectives have supporting content (no missing content), compare the training materials against the instructional design document and against a training checklist, and have the training materials reviewed by editors, testers, subject matter experts (SMEs), and others.

6. Pilot and revise all course materials [placing the cursor over this step displays the following pop up: Try out the course with students from the target audience, solicit feedback, and make any needed improvements.]

Event Text:

The Six Steps of the Instructional Development Process

Developing (building) an outstanding training course from the specifications given in an instructional design document is not a chance event. It requires a disciplined, systematic approach to instructional development that uses a variety of skills that employ various instructional analyses, writing, and micro-design tasks. The outcome of instructional development is the final course deliverables—typically, the final training course consisting of all course materials ready for publishing or delivery.

Move your mouse pointer over each of the five steps of instructional development in the graphic below to learn more.

[Insert graphic here.]

Note: Throughout this module, the terms *topic* and *lesson* are used interchangeably. They both refer to the smallest instructional sequence in a course that typically has an introduction; lesson content, activities, and exercises; and a summary.

After you have moved your mouse pointer over each step and read the information, click Next to continue.

Module 1: Topic 1	Event Type and Description:	**Screen # 3**
	Text and graphic and link that pops up a window	

Event Graphic(s): Graphic of a hierarchical analysis with several levels in it.

Event Text:

Step 1: Analyze the Objectives to Determine All Enabling Content

During instructional design, instructional designers analyze the training requirements and create high-level course plans or blueprints.

During development, these plans are passed on to instructional developers who analyze the objectives and continue drilling down the instructional and content analyses to determine the complete body of detailed information that must be taught to achieve the topic's objectives. During this step, all of the enabling information—every concept, fact, principle, structure, classification, process, and procedure required to master the objective—must be identified.

Note: For detailed information on how to perform instructional and content analyses, see Part 2, "Creating Outstanding Instructional Designs" in my companion book, *Instructional Design—Step by Step: Nine Easy Steps for Designing Lean, Effective, and Motivational Instruction*.

After you have clicked the link and read the information, click Next to continue.

...

[Middle pages of script omitted for brevity]

...

Module 1: Topic 1	Event Type and Description: Checkpoint Question: Multiple Choice – Multiple Answers	**Screen # 27**

Event Graphic(s): Standard checkpoint graphic/background

Event Text:

Check Your Understanding (1 of 3)

In addition to validating the course materials, quality checking a course consists of which of the following activities? (Select all that apply.)

X A. Performing a professional edit of all materials by professional editors for grammar, style, legal and trademark issues, and compliance with any organizational standards.

___ B. Piloting the course on the target audience and evaluating the attainment of course objectives and soliciting feedback

X C. Performing an accessibility review to ensure that the course complies with accessibility requirements for the disabled

X D. Testing the navigation, links, and interactive features of online courses to ensure that they are functioning properly

X E. Having the course reviewed by peers and technical experts for a final check on course integrity, instructional effectiveness, and technical accuracy

___ F. Revising the course to make needed improvements that were uncovered by the course pilots and peer and subject matter expert reviews

Correct feedback: That is correct!

Incorrect feedback: That is incorrect. The correct answer is A, C, D, and E.

Select your answer, then click Evaluate. When you are finished, click Next to continue.

Module 1: Topic 1	Event Type and Description:	**Screen # 28**
	Checkpoint Question: True/False	

Event Graphic(s): Standard checkpoint graphic/background

Event Text:

Check Your Understanding (2 of 3)

_T_ True or false? Piloting the course is trying out the training on the target audience in preliminary training sessions and soliciting feedback using written assessments, interviews, surveys, or other evaluation techniques to see how well the course achieved its objectives, where improvements need to be made, and how well students liked the course.

Correct feedback: Correct! This statement is true.

Incorrect feedback: Actually, this statement is true.

Select your answer, then click Evaluate. When you are finished, click Next to continue.

Module 1: Topic 1	Event Type and Description:	**Screen # 29**
	Checkpoint Question: True/False	

Event Graphic(s): Standard checkpoint graphic/background

Event Text:

Check Your Understanding (3 of 3)

_T_ True or false? Instructional developers are micro-instructional designers.

Correct feedback: Correct! This statement is true. Instructional development is a continuation of the instructional design process and a refinement of the instructional design. Developers must know how to perform many of the same design activities and techniques that instructional designers must know. However, they typically perform them at a lower level in the course, within the confines of the individual course modules, topics, and activities that were previously defined and sequenced in the instructional design document.

Incorrect feedback: Actually, this statement is true. Instructional development is a continuation of the instructional design process and a refinement of the instructional design. Developers must know how to perform many of the same design activities and techniques that instructional designers must know. However, they typically perform them at a lower level in the course, within the confines of the individual course modules, topics, and activities that were previously defined and sequenced in the instructional design document.

Select your answer, then click Evaluate. When you are finished, click Next to continue.

Module 1: Topic 1	Event Type and Description:	**Screen # 30**
	Topic Summary	

Event Graphic(s): Standard topic summary graphic/background

Event Text:

Topic Summary – Overview of How to Develop Training

This topic presented an overview of the instructional development process. It described the major activities involved in developing training, including analyzing topic objectives to determine all of the enabling content for a topic; classifying information into its type; designing information presentations that match the information's type; creating exercises and other instructional events; finalizing the sequence of materials for a topic; creating scripts for technology-based training; performing a quality check on the training materials; and piloting and revising the course materials.

[*Note to courseware engineer:* numbers in square brackets, such as [2], in the Topic Summary indicate the target screen for the hypertext link.]

You should now be able to:

- List the six steps of the instructional development process. [2]
- For each of the following steps in the development process, state the purpose of that step, describe how it is carried out at a high level, and explain why that step is important:
    1. Analyze the objectives to determine all enabling content. [3]
    2. Classify information into its type and create corresponding instructional presentations. [10]
    3. Create the remaining instructional events and finalize the topic. [16]
    4. Create scripts (for technology-based training) [19]
    5. Perform a quality check on the training materials. [24]
    6. Pilot and revise all course materials. [25]
- Describe how instructional development is a continuation and refinement of the instructional design. [26]

If you do not feel confident performing any of these objectives, click the objective to jump to the relevant part of the course. Then click Topic Summary to return to this page.

Click Next to continue to the next topic, or click Menu to return to the previous menu.

Appendix B. Example of a Content Analysis

2 Fundamental network concepts

2.1 Networking concepts

2.1.1 Definition of a network

2.1.1.1 Collection of interconnected hosts that share information

2.1.1.1.1 Systems interconnected with wires or fibers

2.1.1.1.2 Wires and fibers are attached to system adapter cards and other network components (hubs, routers, and switches)

2.1.1.1.3 Signals are transmitted through the wires using specific hardware and software protocols (data packaging and signaling standards)

2.1.1.1.4 Data moves through the physical network using these network protocols

2.1.2 Network control

2.1.2.1 Why network control is necessary

2.1.2.2 Types of network control

2.1.2.2.1 Hierarchical network (e.g., RTLL, CSAM, BRL/TRU)

2.1.2.2.1.1 One central host that controls the entire network

2.1.2.2.1.2 One host (system) within the network controls all data flow across the network

2.1.2.2.1.3 Requires adapter cards

2.1.2.2.2 Peer-to-peer network (TCP/IP, BDL, ZAQ201, ZPPN)

2.1.2.2.2.1 All the hosts in the network are equal (peers to each other) and equally control the network

2.1.2.2.2.2 No central controlling host required; each peer has its own network control program

2.1.2.2.2.3 Network control program must be running in each peer

2.1.2.2.2.4 SS/6000Z SPs are peer-to-peer

2.1.2.2.2.5 Requires adapter cards

2.1.2.2.3 Net-centric network (e.g., GGL, frame relay)

2.1.2.2.3.1 Does not require a host

2.1.2.2.3.2 No network operating system

2.1.2.2.3.3 Any host can be attached to this type of network

2.1.2.2.3.4 Requires some kind of box to attach to the network (e.g., 9125, router)

2.1.3 Network cabling [how to recognize cable type and connector]

2.1.3.1 Why you need to know about network cables

2.1.3.1.1 Each topology specifies valid cable types

2.1.3.1.2 To check the physical integrity of the cable and connector

2.1.3.2 Types of network cables

2.1.3.2.1 Type 1

2.1.3.2.1.1 Best wire but bulky and expensive

2.1.3.2.1.2 Black box connector (like the old token ring)

2.1.3.2.2 Type 5 (STP: Shielded Twisted Pair)

2.1.3.2.2.1 Next best wire but fairly expensive
2.1.3.2.2.2 RJ-45 connector
2.1.3.2.3 UTP: Unshielded twisted pair
2.1.3.2.3.1 Cheap but susceptible to noise
2.1.3.2.3.2 RJ-45 connector
2.1.3.2.4 Coax
2.1.3.2.4.1 Strong and shielded but uncommon (used mainly for thin net)
2.1.3.2.4.2 Requires termination
2.1.3.2.4.2.1 Termination requires 50 Ohm terminators
2.1.3.2.4.3 BNC
2.1.3.2.5 Fiber
2.1.3.2.5.1 Fastest and most expensive but most reliable
2.1.3.2.5.2 Two kinds
2.1.3.2.5.2.1 Multi-mode
2.1.3.2.5.2.1.1 Bigger fiber but slower speed
2.1.3.2.5.2.1.2 Usually an LED driver
2.1.3.2.5.2.2 Single-mode
2.1.3.2.5.2.2.1 Thinner but faster speeds
2.1.3.2.5.2.2.2 Laser (avoid looking at the fiber to prevent eye damage)
2.1.3.2.5.3 ST-ST connection?
2.1.4 Network topologies
2.1.4.1 Network topologies
2.1.4.1.1 Ring (e.g., cash register store loop)
2.1.4.1.1.1 Shielded twisted-pair cabling
2.1.4.1.1.2 Rules [get from LAN concepts Redbook]
2.1.4.1.1.2.1 Distance
2.1.4.1.1.2.2 Number of connections
2.1.4.1.1.2.3 Number of hosts per segment
2.1.4.1.2 Bus (e.g., Ethernet)
2.1.4.1.2.1 Coax cabling
2.1.4.1.2.2 T-connectors
2.1.4.1.2.3 Terminators
2.1.4.1.2.4 Rules [get from LAN concepts Redbook]
2.1.4.1.2.4.1 Distance
2.1.4.1.2.4.2 Number of connections
2.1.4.1.2.4.3 Number of hosts per segment
2.1.4.1.3 Star (e.g., twisted-pair Ethernet with hub or twisted-pair token ring with hub)
2.1.4.1.3.1 Shielded or unshielded twisted pair cabling
2.1.4.1.3.2 Hub
2.1.4.1.3.3 Rules [get from LAN concepts Redbook]
2.1.4.1.3.3.1 Distance
2.1.4.1.3.3.2 Number of connections
2.1.4.1.3.3.3 Number of hosts per segment
2.1.4.1.4 Star-ring (e.g., token ring)
2.1.4.1.4.1 Type 1 cable, Type 5 cable, or shielded twisted-pair cabling

2.1.4.1.4.2 One or more MAUs and/or CAUs
  2.1.4.1.4.2.1 Access ports
  2.1.4.1.4.2.2 Ring in and ring out (interconnect MAUs or CAUs)
2.1.4.1.4.3 Rules [get from LAN concepts Redbook]
  2.1.4.1.4.3.1 Distance
  2.1.4.1.4.3.2 Number of connections
  2.1.4.1.4.3.3 Number of hosts per segment
  2.1.4.1.4.3.4 Speed
2.1.4.1.5 Exercise: Validating customer LAN configurations

2.1.5 ISO model
2.1.5.1 The ISO model and how it functions
  2.1.5.1.1 What is the ISO model?
  2.1.5.1.1.1 Was an attempt to standardize the network industry to allow interoperability of networking hardware
  2.1.5.1.2 Why understand the ISO model?
  2.1.5.1.2.1 To understand how the network protocols (such as TCP/IP) function (see below for detailed discussion of network protocols)
  2.1.5.1.2.2 To understand how routers and bridges function
  2.1.5.1.3 ISO model has 7 layers
  2.1.5.1.3.1 Level 1: Physical Layer
    2.1.5.1.3.1.1 Physical network interface
    2.1.5.1.3.1.2 Has the bit encoding and synchronization
    2.1.5.1.3.1.3 Has the electrical and mechanical specifications (e.g., the ISO model specifies that token ring use the standard 802.5 electrical and physical specification)
  2.1.5.1.3.2 Level 2: Data link layer
    2.1.5.1.3.2.1 Station-to-station information transfer
    2.1.5.1.3.2.2 Error detection with optional error recovery
  2.1.5.1.3.3 Level 3: Network layer
    2.1.5.1.3.3.1 Network addressing and routing
    2.1.5.1.3.3.2 Optional flow control
  2.1.5.1.3.4 Level 4: Transport layer
    2.1.5.1.3.4.1 N to N information transport
    2.1.5.1.3.4.2 The interface between the lower communication layers and the upper communication layers
  2.1.5.1.3.5 Level 5: Session layer
    2.1.5.1.3.5.1 Synchronization of data exchange
    2.1.5.1.3.5.2 Regulates the send and receive of data flow
  2.1.5.1.3.6 Level 6: Presentation layer
    2.1.5.1.3.6.1 Presentation of data in a manner that can be understood by both sender and receiver
  2.1.5.1.3.7 Level 7: Application layer
    2.1.5.1.3.7.1 The interface between the communication functions and the actual application
    2.1.5.1.3.7.2 Has direct end-user services such as FTP, mail, telnet, and SNMP

2.1.5.1.4 How the 7 layers communicate with each other
　2.1.5.1.4.1 Ports
　　2.1.5.1.4.1.1
　2.1.5.1.4.2 Sockets
　　2.1.5.1.4.2.1
2.1.5.1.5 Examples of how each layer of the ISO model can be implemented in practice (e.g., Level 1 can be handled through a token ring or an Ethernet adapter card) [IBM wall chart is available showing layers and how they can be implemented]
2.1.5.1.6 How data flows (up and down through the layers) from end-user to end-user through a network that uses the ISO model (end-to-end communication)
2.1.5.2 Software suites that use the ISO model
　2.1.5.2.1 Definition: A software suite is ISO compliant software that defines how data is physically and logically moved across the network to preserve the data's integrity
　2.1.5.2.2 Each software suite implements the ISO model (all 7 layers)
　2.1.5.2.3 TCP/IP
　　2.1.5.2.3.1 How TCP/IP functions in the ISO model
　　　2.1.5.2.3.1.1 Layers 1 & 2 are the IP part (physical transport)
　　　　2.1.5.2.3.1.1.1 IP is considered a connectionless protocol
　　　　　2.1.5.2.3.1.1.1.1 No data or error recovery (data recovery and error recovery is left to higher network layers)
　　　　　2.1.5.2.3.1.1.1.2 Does not care what physical layer is used (e.g., token ring or Ethernet)
　　　　　2.1.5.2.3.1.1.1.3 Packets can be received in random order and are reassembled in proper order at the transport level
　　　　2.1.5.2.3.1.1.2 IP packets
　　　　2.1.5.2.3.1.1.3 IP addressing
　　　　2.1.5.2.3.1.1.4 Subnet masking
　　　　2.1.5.2.3.1.1.5 Routing and routing tables
　　　2.1.5.2.3.1.2 Layers 3 through 7 are the software component parts (FTP, UDP, SNMP, mail, telnet, etc.)
　2.1.5.2.4 Other software suites
2.1.6 Types of networks
　2.1.6.1 LANS
　　2.1.6.1.1 Definition of LAN (Local Area Network)
　　　2.1.6.1.1.1 Geographically small network made up of one or more network topologies (including two or more of the same topology)
　　　2.1.6.1.1.2 Simple (one topography only) to complex (many different topographies interconnected on the same LAN)
　　2.1.6.1.2 Segments
　　　2.1.6.1.2.1 Smallest physical unit of a network that makes up a network in-and-of itself
　　　2.1.6.1.2.2 Has one topology
　　　2.1.6.1.2.3 Segments can be interconnected through bridges and routers to form more complex LANs

2.1.6.1.3 Bridges
2.1.6.1.3.1 A network component that is used to connect both similar and dissimilar LAN segments together to form a larger network
2.1.6.1.3.2 Are relatively "dumb" network components that pass all network traffic passively
2.1.6.1.3.3 Function only in the physical layer (layers 1 and 2 in the ISO model)
2.1.6.1.3.4 Two kinds of bridging
  2.1.6.1.3.4.1 Transparent bridging
    2.1.6.1.3.4.1.1
  2.1.6.1.3.4.2 Source route bridging
    2.1.6.1.3.4.2.1
2.1.6.1.3.5 ARP/RARP Tables
  2.1.6.1.3.5.1 Takes the network address (e.g., IP address) and maps it to a MAC address
    2.1.6.1.3.5.1.1 Media Access Control (MAC) address
      2.1.6.1.3.5.1.1.1 Physical address of the adapter card
2.1.6.1.4 Routers
2.1.6.1.4.1 Are more intelligent network components
2.1.6.1.4.2 Function from the physical layer (layers 1 and 2) through the transmission layer (layer 3)
2.1.6.1.4.3 Have knowledge of the entire network through dynamic routing tables (see IP discussion for detail on routing tables)
  2.1.6.1.4.3.1 Can intelligently forward data on to its destination
2.1.6.1.4.4 Have more filtering capability (e.g., can screen out traffic that is not destined for a given network)
2.1.6.1.4.5 Have their own operating system
  2.1.6.1.4.5.1 RIP
    2.1.6.1.4.5.1.1 An older technology
    2.1.6.1.4.5.1.2 Susceptible to network slowdowns because it does not handle network traffic efficiently
  2.1.6.1.4.5.2 OFPF (Open Fastest Path First)
    2.1.6.1.4.5.2.1 Better, newer technology
    2.1.6.1.4.5.2.2 Determined through routing tables
2.1.6.1.5 Backbones
2.1.6.1.5.1 A segment that is only used to connect other segments together
2.1.6.1.5.2 Does not have a host connection
2.1.6.1.5.3 Interconnected to other segments through a bridge or router
2.1.6.1.6 Types of LANs
  2.1.6.1.6.1 Token ring
    2.1.6.1.6.1.1 Topology
      2.1.6.1.6.1.1.1 Star hub
      2.1.6.1.6.1.1.2 Star ring
    2.1.6.1.6.1.2 Physical layer protocol
      2.1.6.1.6.1.2.1 Token ring goes through five phases when getting on the ring

2.1.6.1.6.1.2.1.1 Phase 1: Test the adapter card

2.1.6.1.6.1.2.1.2 Phase 2: Sends the phantom 5 voltage to the MAU or the CAU to open the relay

2.1.6.1.6.1.2.1.3 Phase 3: Determine if anyone else is out on the ring

2.1.6.1.6.1.2.1.4 Phase 4: Determine the active monitor (lowest MAC address)

2.1.6.1.6.1.2.1.5 Phase 5: Rebuild the network and determine who nearest upstream neighbor is

[The analysis continues from here.]

Bibliography

Clark, Ruth C. *Developing Technical Training: A Structured Approach for Developing Classroom and Computer-Based Instructional Materials, 2nd Edition.* Washington, D.C.: International Society for Performance Improvement, 1999.

Hoffman, John S. *Instructional Design—Step by Step: Nine Easy Steps for Designing Lean, Effective, and Motivational Instruction*. Bloomington, IN: iUniverse, 2013.

Strunk, Jr, William and E. B. White. *The Elements of Style, 4th edition.* New York: Longman, 2000.

Index

graphics 72, 95, 124

group discussions 108

grouping. *See* sensory perception, grouping

H

horizon. *See* sensory perception, horizon

Horn, Robert xi, 44, 50, 153

I

if-then-else statement. *See* structured-English outlines, if-then-else statement

improving the course. *See* training, revising

indicator behaviors 36

information
sequencing. *See* also structuring the course

information types. *See* taxonomies, learning, information types (Horn); *See* taxonomies, learning, information types (Horn)

instructional analysis 28, 38
analyzing complex procedures. *See* procedure, analyzing complex

instructional design. *See* also training; learning
blended learning. *See* blended learning
delivery system. *See* instructional delivery system
for computer application training. *See* computer application training
identifying enabling content. *See* enabling content
introductions. *See* introductions
layout and design principles. *See* layout and design principles
quiz. *See* exam
structuring the course. *See* structuring the course
summaries. *See* summaries

target audience. *See* training requirements

test. *See* exam

training requirements. *See* training requirements

instructional design document 10, 13, 110, 128
course fit into curriculum. *See* course prerequisites
course prerequisites. *See* course prerequisites

instructional designer 20, 126, 130, 131

instructional development
a continuation of instructional design 21
analytical nature of 5
definition of 3
goals of 4
importance of 5
necessary skills for 6
output of 4
overview of 9
participants in 4
steps of 10

instructional events 10, 17, 19, 108, 112, 128
specifications for 109

instructional game 17, 108

instructional lesson. *See* lesson; structuring the course

instructional modules. *See* structuring the course

instructional objectives 10, 11, 19, 28, 126
analyzing 11, 27
analyzing attitudinal 36
analyzing knowledge 33
analyzing skill 32
classifying into SKA type 31

instructional strategies 16, 50

instructional topics. *See* structuring the course

instructional units. *See* structuring the course

instructor-led training 110

interactivity. *See* also instructional
    events

IT specialist 4

J

job analysis. *See* instructional analysis

job outcomes. *See* also training
    requirements

job skills. *See* also job outcomes

K

key information 129, 174

knowledge
  key. *See* information, key

knowledge (as part of SKA taxonomy)
    29

L

label statement (in structured-English
    outlines). *See* structured-English
    outlines, label statement

layering. *See* information layering

layering information 129, 173

lean instruction. *See* training, lean

learning. *See* also training
  adult learning principles. see adult
    learning principles
  cognitive encoding techniques. *See*
    cognition, cognitive encoding
    techniques
  examples. *See* examples
  exercises. *See* exercises
  memory. *See* memory
  needs analysis. *See* instructional
    analysis
  pace. *See* training, pace
  practice. *See* practice
  relevance. *See* learning, motivation
  sensory perception. *See* sensory
    perception
  simulations. *See* training, simulations

  taxonomies. *See* taxonomies, learning;
    See taxonomies, learning

learning management system 142

lesson 11, 15, 114

M

memory 148
  chunking. *See* chunking

memory strategies 93

mentoring 109

motivation. *See* learning, motivation

motivational incentives 89

mysterious information 179

N

needs analysis. *See* also instructional
    analysis

new terms 179

non-examples 77

note statement (in structured-English
    outlines). *See* structured-English
    outlines, note statement

O

objectives. *See* instructional objectives;
    See instructional objectives

observation 108

organization 93, 156, 183

P

parallel structure in lists 176

performance gap. *See* instructional
    analysis

performance test. *See* exam

person-on-the-street test 152
  examples for conceptual information
    153
  examples for process information 155
  examples for structural information
    154

soliciting feedback 139

stage, as part of a process 70

stimulus. *See* also learning, stimulus
position of. *See* sensory perception,
stimulus position

structure 14, 48, 94, 154
teaching 95

structuring information 18, 49, 111,
112, 129
guidelines for 113

style guide. *See* lesson, style guide

subject-matter expert (SME) 20, 126,
130, 131

subject-matter experts (SMEs). *See*
instructional analysis, working with
SMEs during

subroutine statement (in structured-
English outlines). *See* structured-
English outlines, subroutine
statement

summary 17, 108

T

table 59, 72

target audience. *See* training
requirements

task analysis. *See* instructional analysis;
See instructional analysis

taxonomies, learning
information types (Horn) 10, 13, 14,
15, 44, 153
SKA (Skill, Knowledge, Attitude) 13, 28

technology-based training. *See* training,
technology-based

template 109, 114

test. *See* exam

topic. *See* lesson

training. *See* also learning
analysis. *See* instructional analysis
audience. *See* training requirements
blended learning. *See* blended learning

delivery system. *See* instructional
delivery system
examples. *See* examples
exercises. *See* practice
introductions. *See* introductions
layout and design principles. *See*
layout and design principles
lesson. *See* lesson
mistakes. *See* twenty common training
mistakes rating sheet
module. *See* structuring the course
needs analysis. *See* needs analysis
objectives. *See* instructional objectives
overviews. *See* overviews
performing a quality check on 10, 19,
126
practice. *See* practice
prerequisites. *See* course prerequisites
quiz. *See* exam
rating. *See* twenty common training
mistakes rating sheet
revising 11, 20, 140
strategies. *See* instructional strategies;
See instructional strategies
structuring. *See* structuring the course
summaries. *See* summaries
target audience. *See* training
requirements
technology-based 10
test. *See* exam
topic. *See* structuring the course
unit. *See* structuring the course
validating the materials for 19, 126

training analysis. *See* instructional
analysis

training audience. *See* training
requirements

training design document. *See*
instructional design document

training pilot 11, 20, 138

training requirements. *See* also content
analysis; instructional analysis

transitional slides. *See* slide, transitional

transitions 160

type size 183

typography. *See* sensory perception, typography

U

user interface
  layout and design. *See* layout and design principles

V

validating the materials. *See* training, validating the materials for
vertical alignment lines 181
virtual world 109
visual balance 180

W

word processor. *See* instructional analysis, word processor use in
writers. *See* content developers
writing skills 111